ABANDON HOPE!

The Way to Fulfillment...

D1593496

you —

as **Buddha**
as **God**

as **you** —

ABANDON HOPE!

The Way to Fulfillment...

by Justin F. Stone

Good Karma Publishing
Fort Yates

GOOD KARMA PUBLISHING, Inc., Publisher
P.O. Box 511
Fort Yates, ND 58538

Printed in the United States of America by BookMasters, Inc., Mansfield, OH

First Good Karma Publishing, Inc. edition: February 1989
Second printing: November 1989
Third printing: December 1991
Fourth printing: December 2000

Original drawings - Justin F. Stone
Photographs on pp. 12, 52, 80 - Kimberly Grant, used with permission
Photo transfer of other photographs from Justin F. Stone's personal collection - Bruce D. Wendt
Design and layout - Jean Katus

♲ *Text printed on recycled paper*

Library of Congress Catalog Number 88-83480

ISBN 0-9620812-2-1

Dedicated to
PAUL REPS
who has enriched my bread
for more than 35 years

Roshi Joshu Sasaki

It is not what the Teacher TEACHES that is important, but what he IS.

CONTENTS

Srimata Gayatri Devi

FOREWORD

Srimata Gayatri Devi is the Spiritual Head of the beautiful Ananda Ashrams in La Crescenta, California, and Cohasset, Massachusetts. One of the relatively few female Gurus in the world, she was the disciple of Swami Parmenanda, whose Master, the great Vivekananda, was a direct disciple of Paramahansa Ramakrishna. Thus Mataji, as she is affectionately called, is in the direct line of descent of the spiritual giant of modern times, Ramakrishna, and she perpetuates the devotion to Divine Mother that is characteristic of this lineage.

Excerpts from Gayatri Devi's Christmas Address Cohasset, December 16, 1973

In every one of us there is a vital need and that need is for something other than what our everyday life brings. Sometimes we can be jubilant, and then we are downcast; this is a common experience until we have touched in our own lives that which is always awaiting us...The real need, the yearning need, for all souls, is God. And we may not realize this, we may become so engrossed in our lives of many affairs and interests, but all the while this is missing, and therefore a time comes when we recognize our own need and we reach out for God. You see, if this did not happen to us, we would go through life, our entire life, just touching and not touching, finding and not finding.

Christmas is here again, and for me each Christmas is an experience when one becomes identified with what Christ represents, with what Mother represents, with what this relationship represents. Aren't we all children of God? Aren't we all born of Divine Mother? Isn't our relationship an everlasting one? Is this something we just take for granted and forget? So we become identified with Mary, with Jesus, with what they represent to us. And what is the result? You feel such love, you become love...You become alive...Divine Mother is saying to us, "You have come. I have been waiting for you." She is greeting you. And at that moment, when you feel like this, you become the Christ child...

In our lives there should be the practice of always blending the outer and the inner. When the outer becomes top-heavy, the inner is crushed. And when that which is inside is allowed to come forward, all the outer takes on new light. In our highest moment, the mystical moment, we have the realization of who dwells within us, who has given us life and the capacity to be. That is our highest moment, and we should seek it. Then you will say, "Of course, outside and inside are all one. God and man are not separate. My religious life and my daily life, are all one." What has happened to you? Because of your inner realization, all has become God for you. This is what it means to touch the Center...

We all have the right, the equal right, to reach out and have the best and the highest. So why shouldn't you have your God? Why shouldn't you be so very close? But you are the one who has to decide upon this. Don't say, "Life is too busy...I must give service to others; I must take care of all my needs." You are neglecting something that also needs to be taken care of. Your God wants you. He wants your company. He wants to draw you close. So you have every right to sit still. You have every right to take these precious moments when you can be aloof from all other ties, and become united...It will happen if you reach out. You will be flooded with joy when you realize that He is dwelling right inside of you, enshrined in your own being.

We should touch, we should come so very close that our own being can melt in the other Being. Don't be afraid. You're going to die? At a certain point death is life. Because you have not died you have not started to live. You are holding back all the time, frightened. And when you learn to let go you realize: what dies in you needs to die, so that what must live can be born in you...If you hear the slightest call, you should be ready to respond. But you say, "No, wait. I have other things to do. I'll come later." You should say instead, "I'll come. I'm here. Take me." Then what? Am I lost to the world? Of course not. Why separate God and the world? They are one, only we don't yet know it.

Let us learn that it is unity, oneness, that we are all seeking. But it must begin with you, in your relationship with God. If we do it, we find a meaning to our life. When our union with the Source has taken place, there is our fulfillment. Actually our work begins then. Then we can give more; we can share. Let Christmas help us to become established in our relationship with God. Let it be so for every one of us.

THE AUTHOR IN JAPAN during a two-day ceremony in Nara.

The above picture is included for the benefit of those students who have remarked disappointedly: "Oh, you look just like a regular American!"

If a teacher must rely on robes, assumed religious names, and other trappings to gain respect, he's a teacher in name only.

INTRODUCTION

T he mystery of Being is the matter that concerns us all. Next to the activity of Being, politics is child's play, business is a superficial game, and war is the squawking of alley cats. Perhaps the Scientist and the Artist, each in his own way, is attempting to plumb the Mystery. When Man is in tune with his own Being, he is content and joyous. When out of tune in the whole physico-mental organism, he is consumed by insatiable desires.

And so we have religions, priestcraft, Gurus, Saints and Aints (as Paul Reps would say), and others about whom I am writing in this book. Since the book is one-third reminiscence and two-thirds spiritual commentary (and, sometimes, criticism), perhaps it will not be everybody's cup of tea. I enjoyed writing it, and felt many of the things should be said, but that doesn't mean everybody will enjoy reading it.

Two different sides of Japan are presented in the book, and the author has lived in both parts. Obviously, he prefers the traditional as opposed to the helter-skelter "modern." In writing about the Gurus and the two missionary religions from Japan, the author is dealing with some people he respects and who mean a great deal to him; yet "truth," as he sees it, must be spoken.

The chapters called "The Growth of Certainty" and "Poems of Inner Meaning" (poems of spiritual experience) obviously are personal in nature. It is to be hoped that they are not too intense or too personal, and that those with different tastes will realize there are many flavors.

I have included Srimata Gayatri Devi's inspiring Christmas talk in a foreword as I believe it touches on some of the subject matter in this book and because I want to make it more widely available. Those who have seen Mataji's serene and beautiful face do not have to ask if she knows an inner contentment.

The greatest moments of my life have been spent with religious or spiritual figures. A Saint is, by definition, joyous. A gloomy Saint or spiritual teacher would be a contradiction. If one is out of tune with Being, he has nothing to pass along

1

to others. Where there is the Religious Heart, that is where I want to be. To me there is no separate religion; there is only Religion with a capital "R." Whether we speak of "Seeing your own True Nature" or of "Realizing God," the meaning is the same. Metaphysical questions and doubts expressed as to whether God exists or not are just amusements, ways to titillate the mind. They have nothing to do with Truth, and it is only through Truth — *being* it, not talking about it — that we can manifest the Joy of Being. It is true that many Churches — and some teachers — attempt only to pacify and to offer spiritual tranquilizers. In the long run this is damaging and does nothing to heighten Spirituality, which I define as "Identification with the Real." So-called "Spiritual Life" can become abject bondage; it is all up to the aspirant, and seeking the True, living the True, takes courage.

I have enjoyed my contact with Maharishi, with George Ohsawa, with Rammurti Mishra, with the fine people of Sekai Kyusei Kyo, with Roshi Sasaki and beautiful Ogata-Fujin of the Zen world, and with Reverend Hayashi and family and my "brother," Reverend Takahashi, of the Tenrikyo "Joyous Life" Church. There are so many others, not named, in whom I have discerned the seed of Spirituality, and in whose presence I have been happy. One day I would like to write a book about the great present-day Karma Yogi, Swami Krishnanand, of Baroda, India. Perhaps, at a different time, I could speak of the Island Hermitage in Ceylon, one of several communities in which the Buddha's original practice is being perpetuated. And, certainly, T'ai Chi Ch'uan Master and great Scholar Professor Wen-Shan Huang is a friend from whom I have learned many spiritual lessons.

So I have enjoyed writing this book, but really have no idea whether the reader, too, will enjoy it. I ask that he or she see it through eyes attempting to focus on the True. Beyond that, I can only ask for: Peace to All Beings.

CHAPTER 1

ABANDON HOPE!

"**A**bandon Hope, all ye who enter here!"
This would appear to be the opposite of everything we believe in, the deathblow to our expectation of living a full and fulfilled life. But it isn't. Quite the contrary, it is the way to wake up and come to life, to live the beauty of the present and to know, with gratitude, the Joy of Being. Only by abandoning hope for the future can we know life in the present.

This is a desire world. We are here, in our present form, because of our desires and the habit energies they have created. These habit energies are the cause and we are the result, and our reactions every minute of our lives are building new causes, which must, some time, have effect. We are here vainly trying to fulfill our desires, gasping and struggling as we pursue the impossible task — trying desperately to avoid pain, to experience pleasure, and to hang on to and repeat what has been pleasurable. Most of us are caught up in this pleasure-pain syndrome, and so we make plans, always hoping tomorrow will bring fulfillment and release from endless pressures. We hope against hope, that tomorrow, or next year, things will be better. Yet, "not-seeking" is the Way.

This is our world, and, to most people, the very possibility that there might be other worlds, other levels of consciousness, does not exist. Yet, Sages tell us the number of worlds and planes of Being are infinite. Still, in all our anxiety, we insist on remaining here, on clinging to our misery, creating attachments that go on life after life.

Does this mean "reincarnation," a much misused term? What is it that comes back, an entity named John Jones or Minoru Watanabe? Hardly. But it is inevitable that causes have effects, so there will be a future life. Zen calls this "Handing your seat to another," and it is a grave responsibility. Some personality will feel the consequences of what we have sown, and, in truth, that stranger will be ourself. The seed of an apple can only produce an apple tree.

So we pile desire upon desire and plan upon plan. Not content to let the inevitable happen, we try to manipulate what cannot be manipulated. We build on hope and daydream, and, in the wise words of Alice in Wonderland, always have "Jam yesterday, jam tomorrow, but never jam today!" This today never comes for us as we plan for a better tomorrow for ourselves, our children, our grandchildren. Our stock will rise, our ability will suddenly be recognized, we will find the part we've always dreamed of, somebody who appreciates us will finally appear, our boss will begin to sympathize with us, ad infinitum. Does it ever happen? And if we do receive what we had once hoped for, does it satisfy us for long and does it change our lives?

We are not unhappy because of our circumstances; we have these circumstances because we are unhappy and are determined to prolong that unhappiness. How we cling to the very things that cause our suffering! They are what is closest to us, and we are afraid that, if we let go, we will have nothing! Does the compulsive gambler let go the habit that causes endless torment? Not for anything — for family, friends, or reputation. Rather, he "feels" things will be better tomorrow. He lives in the hope of the future, alive in his suffering and afraid of the void, the emptiness, if it were turned off and he had to face himself. The suffering is a narcotic keeping him from ever looking within. Again, in Zen terms, he faces his problem by "whippping the cart and not the horse." Without changing himself he cannot change his circumstances. We each live in a private world created by our own desires and seen through a veil of self-interest. It is pure illusion, but who will believe it? Who will look WITHIN to see that world, knowing the outer is merely a reflection? This requires courage and the Abandonment of Hope. Only by seeing things as they are, without a shred of hope that they will be different, can we get a glimpse of Reality. Otherwise we are always blowing the smoke-dream of illusion, hoping for one result while we experience another.

So Abandon Hope! We are all going to die. Accept that and there is no hope of living on indefinitely. So it no longer poses a problem. We have accepted death as the inevitable concomitant of birth, so we have no hope in that direction and death can no longer threaten us. We have accepted it without hope.

Having abandoned hope of endlessly-prolonged life, let's Abandon Hope of being what we're not. I am bald, I am old, I am unattractive, I do not have any mechanical aptitude —

Bunraku Puppet Master

accept these facts and Abandon Hope that the unchangeable will change, that Cinderella will suddenly appear from an ugly crone, and these facts can no longer hurt us. A Chinese scholar once defined a sage for me as "one who wants spring to follow winter." Not summer to follow winter, or spring to come before winter, but simply spring to follow winter. This is in the nature of things and, being wise, he accords with the nature of things. No hope of changing what is, but joyous compliance with what is. So Abandon Hope that things, somehow, are different from what they are. Do your best and leave the result to the great Law of the Universe. Do not waste time hoping that men will not be cruel, avaricious, and fickle. Work toward helping them to a different end, if you will, and make your motto "each according to his need." But do not hope that what is not so will suddenly become so. The apple seed sprouts only an apple tree, and that only under proper conditions. But isn't an apple tree remarkable? Isn't it expressing life fully? Isn't it miraculous that a seed carries in it a tree, indeed, whole forests of trees? Abandon Hope that it will change and enjoy it for what it is.

A good example of one who Abandons Hope is the man who becomes a monk. Entering the monastery, he leaves the past behind, forgets family, abandons hope of fame, fortune, and fulfillment in the future, and lays the burden down. Of course, I have met many who are not true monks and who had no idea of abandoning hope for the future. Nor were they able to sever ties with the past. They have simply switched their problems, anxieties, and regrets to a different locale. But I am speaking of the true monk who, entering on his calling, abandons everything but the present moment, where there is no room for Hope. And only in that present moment will he find fulfillment. Hence we speak of "sudden enlightenment" — can there be any other kind but in the present? Abandon the past and the future, live fully in the "Now" with no hope of anything, and the "Now" reveals itself, containing in itself both the past and the future. This is true renunciation, and this is Ananda, Joy, the Bliss of what is, not the hope of what might be.

The great Chinese sage, Lao Tzu, spoke of "losing a little each day" — no increment, no hope of gain, only jettisoning of what obscures the present. His follower, Chuang Tzu, wrote about the "Fasting Mind," where we dispose of the artificial and retain the natural, and where we live in the spontaneous and let the habitual die. The Fasting Mind — not feeding on schemes, plans, hopes, recriminations, regrets, but resting in the empty potentiality that is devoid of object. When we rest in pure subjectivity, away from the fields of the senses and the objects of the mind, we are only ourselves. This is Self-Realization. And where is there any hope for the future in such conditions? We are, now. "Hope" is the other side of fear. "Either-or" is the root of suffering. "Neither-nor" is Bliss, the Truth of Buddhism. And, where there is "Neither-nor," what can we hope for?

So, Abandon Hope! And the desire patterns will fade. If I have no hope of winning, I will not play the game. Only in this way can I say, "Thy Will be Done!" The Divine Lila (Play) is beyond comprehension and beyond imagining, but we create our own role in it. Only without hope of return can we truly love; otherwise we are merely bartering. True love is not personal or compartmentalized; if we love, we love all, including ourselves.

The animal mother has no hope of any reward; she is doing what must be done, and each will abandon its young, without hope or wish, when the right time arrives. This is Love, and it is manifestation of the way things are.

When the great Japanese Zen mystic, Hakuin, had his first major enlightenment experience, he said: "After this, looking at things of the world was like seeing the back of my own hand." If everything is included in us, if we've expanded to embrace all, what can we hope for? Autumn follows summer; it is warm in summer and the leaves turn color in autumn. The breeze blows across the waters of the pond and there are waves. When the wind dies down, the water becomes placid. And the same moon is reflected in every river, pond, and ocean.

It feels good to put the burden down. Do we have the courage to do so? Abandoning hope is not abandoning life! It is giving up misery and its causes so we can live more fully (and only in this way can we love — love is not personal but overflowing). Ambition has caused more unrest than almost any other factor. What is meant to come will come without seeking! What is ours is ours — we do not have to hope for it. "No-seeking" is the Way.

"To a mind that is still, the Universe surrenders," says the poet. And to a heart abiding in emptiness, anything is possible — even joyous fulfillment. So muster up the courage — ABANDON HOPE! "You must die to live — in order to arrive at pleasure in everything, desire to have pleasure in nothing. In order to arrive at knowing everything, desire to know nothing."

St. John of the Cross

And then, ABANDON THE ABANDONMENT!

CHAPTER 2

Expansion and Contraction

THE GURU BUSINESS

T he Guru Business is good, and getting better. Almost any teacher, or would-be teacher, from India, Tibet, China, or Japan — and sometimes other Oriental countries — can come to the United States, wearing robes, and immediately acquire a coterie of followers, ready to kiss his feet and gift him with fruit and flowers in the traditional fashion. It makes no difference that these instant disciples have no proof of the authenticity of the teaching, or of the teacher's own merit. The newly-appeared teacher does not have to be an enlightened Master carrying out his Bodhisattva role of saving all beings — the only necessities are that he wear robes, have an Oriental-sounding name, and have something spiritual to sell or give away.

Many Europeans have adopted Oriental names, thus making it possible to get in on the "Yoga" instruction (actually, Hatha Yoga, one-eighth of the total Raja Yoga, is generally all that is taught), the Tibetan Tantra discourses, the guidance in Zen sitting, and the more esoteric but less well-known Oriental disciplines, ranging all the way down to bogus dietary fads. Some Americans have been voyaging to India and Japan to get quick "credentials." The fact that they have been in an Ashram or Temple, and can use a few Sanskrit, Chinese, or Japanese words, is enough to give authenticity to their claims, and pretty soon they have Roshi, Swami, or Baba in front of what were originally prosaic western names. This in no way reflects on the many wonderful disciplines in the Orient; it simply speaks of the gullibility of those here, mostly young, who are desperately seeking for something to believe in and some direction in which to go.

A Krishnamurti who said, "I am not a teacher, and don't believe anything because I tell it to you" is rare. He wore prosaic business suits and obviously didn't want to capitalize on the Guru Business. But neither he, nor anyone else, can stem the tide. Some teachers in India, learning of the bonanza, arrange backing from business people and come here to "look the situation over." They immediately find their own little

13

group. Others leave jobs in the Orient to devote themselves fulltime to the pursuit. And mixed in with the onrushing horde are, undoubtedly, some authentic teachers.

What makes the guru business prosper?

There are several logical reasons for its prosperity, I believe. Young people have been conned by their parents, their schools, their churches, their government, and by the media, and they are hungry for some "Truth." They want to find some meaning to life beyond Consumership, and they want to travel, economically, with neither the Hounds nor the Hares. Early in life they have been told not to lie, and then, two minutes later when the phone rings, have seen their moralizing parent put a finger to his or her lips and whisper, "I'm not here! I'm not here!" Government propaganda has manipulated them as it willed, and they have been told by the Church that playing Bingo is the way to Heaven. Is it any wonder they are desperately seeking some Truth, any Truth? Where they might have hoped to find it in Institutions of Higher Education, they find, instead, that they are relegated to the identity of an IBM card. Only if this card is bent or marred can they attract personal attention, unless they are professional athletes.

Moreover, there is the urge to join, not to be alone. The young people pride themselves on being "non-conformist," so they rush to group with others of the same bent. We might soon have a new bumper sticker saying, "BE A NON-CONFORMIST. EVERYBODY'S DOING IT!"

So this rush to identify, to find some warmth in the company of others, leads them to groups that chant unintelligible sounds, sit in uncomfortable positions, and urge renunciation of the most cherished activities. Nor are these actions harmful in themselves. Deep in the background there is usually legitimate reason for them, if properly understood.

This urge to identify eventually leads to proselytizing. The Guru finds it easy to persuade followers to bring others to the True Teaching, and they become unpaid salesmen, Missionaries of Hope, taking on all the anxieties that such activity brings. To do this, the initiate must lie a little about his own experiences, must exaggerate in order to make the teaching or discipline more attractive. Then, he or she must believe that the True Teacher has been found. This is an outgrowth of "My Dad can lick your Dad!" of early childhood. Why

14

should we give gifts to the Guru, support him, or give him planes to fly so as to bring the teaching to others? Because it is God's Will. (Somebody in the group has a pipeline to Divinity!) Don't we want others to share our bliss? It is not enough that we meditate or practise, as originally urged — we must become a part of the organization to bring tranquillity to others. This is how churches and cults evolve.

There is a very descriptive story that takes place in Hell. A junior devil, second class, has been sent to Earth to look around and see how things are progressing. He quickly returns to Hell, horrified, and obtains an interview with Beelzebub himself.

"Sir!" he sputters. "Something awful has happened! There is a man with a beard walking around on earth, speaking Truth, and people are beginning to listen to him."

The Devil smiles pleasantly, puffing on his pipe but making no comment.

"Sir! You don't realize the seriousness of the situation," continues the distraught junior devil, second class. "Pretty soon all may be lost!"

The Devil removes his pipe slowly, taps it out in the ashtray, and sits back in his swivel chair, hands behind his head.

"Don't worry, son," he counsels. "We'll let it go on a little longer, and when it has progressed far enough, we'll step in and help them to Organize."

So it is easy to see why the young person joins, accepts initiation, willingly suffers painful disciplines, and volunteers, in the name of Non-Conformity and Freedom, to help build an organization where one must conform and take orders. He or she is looking for some Truth, for some Meaning to Living, and for some group to glorify so that he can identify with the Best. And, strangely, such urges are constructive — far better than the terrible economic competitiveness he or she has been taught, or the status-seeking at the expense of others with which that person has been brainwashed. The sad part is that it so often leads to competitiveness of spiritual groups and a desire for affirmation of spiritual status.

The older person usually comes to the Guru for different reasons. He has long since lost the idealism and the youthful confidence that he or she is meant to do Great Things. Instead, he looks for surcease from the everyday tensions and release from the constant need to memorize numbers — bank numbers, telephone numbers, social security numbers, credit card numbers, and others — the very numbers that have come to spell out his identity to the world. Hearing that a particular discipline is a "tranquilizer," or that it will give him energy and help him to sleep, he is prepared to follow the Guru as a sort of psychotherapy. So the Guru, who came to save his soul, changes his approach and promises to bring him rest while making him more efficient (get higher grades, make more money, cope better with other people). The tranquilizing approach is better boxoffice. And very often the older person does find surcease in his new practice, even occasionally remaking his life. There are many Ways, but they all lead in one direction.

It is, thus, not hard to account for the success of Guruji. "Tradition" is the awesome strength he has behind him, and usually the traditions themselves are old and proven. So the Guru takes on the coloration of the discipline, whether he has personally succeeded in it or not. As in every walk of life, we often have bogus salesmen successfully selling authentic merchandise.

Perhaps the most publicized Guru to come to America is Maharishi Mahesh Yogi, teaching "Transcendental Meditation" (TM). It is unclear how he received the title "Maharishi," Mahesh being his family name. Actually, in India, the term Maha Rishi (Great Sage) might be taken as referring to Yogi Vasistha of antiquity, the teacher of the Avatar Rama (teacher of an incarnation of God!) or to present-day Ramana Maharshi, the great Advaitist of Southern India. No one in India would dispute their right to this most prestigious appellation.

Maharishi's "Guru Dev," his beloved teacher, was Shankaracharya (almost a Pope-like title greatly respected by Indians of all faiths) of Nothern India. Maharishi, upon his Master's death, was not chosen to be his successor, and, subsequently, went out on his own, coming to the west unheralded, without followers, and devoid of financial means. His mission was to spread the teaching of the Meditation known as Manasika Japa in India to ten percent of the people of the world, a most ambitious project.

Satya Sai Baba of India has been quoted as calling Maharishi "the $50 Yogi" and saying that "that Mahesh fellow has set true Yoga back 100 years in America." The original notoriety concerning the Beatles and various actors and actresses attracted quite a few people who had an affinity with notoriety, and probably repelled many more who did not look on Yoga (the Science of Divine Union) as part of Show Business. For a long time after the inevitable defection of the Beatles, Maharishi was looked upon as a comic figure, riding in Rolls Royces, sojourning only with the famous, and selling Meditation, with a giggle, on television whenever the opportunity presented itself. This unfortunate turn was more the result of inappropriate advice than the fault of the teacher. In 1962, when plans were being made to raise money by approaching "important people" (as though anyone was unimportant!), this writer stood up in a public meeting and suggested, "You had better examine your motives first." The reception to this remark was mixed, at best.

My own feeling, from having spent a good deal of time with Maharishi in the early years, is that he is a genuinely enlightened teacher. The typical Indian verbosity turns off many who listen to hours of repetitive talk, some wanting a more succinct and disciplined approach. (This was the reaction of a great Chinese teacher I took to hear him.) But I believe Maharishi has a legitimate, well-defined mission in the world. While it now seems hardly likely he will bring ten percent of the world's population to Transcendental Meditation, I do feel he has imbedded the possibility of meditating in the consciousness of many. And what he is teaching is very valid, though somewhat incomplete (from a Yogic standpoint) in its present form.

Unlike the true Zen Master, who aims at bringing complete enlightenment to a few, Maharishi's mission seems to be to start much of suffering humanity on the road to spiritual progress, through meditation, so that, in some future life, they will take up the task and progress further along the Way to Self-Realization. This is a laudable aim, to make a beginning with many rather than bringing a few to fruition.

If it had not been for the ill-conceived publicity and misguided advice, Maharishi might have progressed more rapidly toward his goal. Instead of small groups of followers here and there, there might have been a mass movement toward meditation in many parts of the world. As it is, the number of practising followers in this country might approximate the audience Billy Graham would draw in any large city on any one night.

Nevertheless, progress is being made, particularly in the Universities of the West. It is true that there are grave questions about "selling a Mantra" (a name of God) and about initiation and profit-sharing by traveling instructors, who are not themselves enlightened teachers. (Often they fail to fulfill the instructions to check meditations after the money has been paid and the initiation given, resulting in some initiates having had bad experiences, with no one to help them.) The logical answer to this, however, would be that it is necessary to reach a far wider group, in all parts of the world, than Maharishi could personally hope to do. Perhaps this is somewhat analogous to Jesus sending out his disciples on their Ministry of Healing; only time will tell us.

It is my personal feeling that Maharishi really wants nothing for himself — neither personal aggrandizement nor riches. So, while we may quarrel with the method (in Spiritual exercises the means IS the end, and the wrong means to an end is not permissible), Maharishi's purpose and the practice he is offering are both laudable.

Other Gurus, some admirable and some looking for fame and fortune, will continue to turn up long into the future, I believe, and, along with some foreign church teachings that are infiltrating America, they probably represent a turn away from stifling materialism. Those who come from India will all be called "Swami," despite the fact that only an initiate into the order of Sanyasi is truly a Swami. It is not merely a term of respect. And a Sanyasi is a renunciate, one who has forsaken home, family, and financial means. So, when we hear of a teacher who is accumulating presents, buying cars and planes, and living in luxurious homes, called "Swami," it is ludicrous. Actually, almost all great teachers in India's long history have been renunciates, usually wandering mendicants. The Buddha, who was a Prince of a Kingdom in Northeast India, left family and inheritance to become a wandering ascetic, almost starving to death on the way to his Enlightenment. And Yogi Vasistha, Ramana Maharshi, Sankara, Ramakrishna — none of these were Householders. The idea of a rich Sanyasi, or of a Perfect Master rolling in wealth (and perhaps suffering from the psychosomatic disorders that go with it), is unthinkable to the Indian — but apparently not to the seeking public in this country. "The son of God hath not where to lay his head," has made little impression on the laity, nor on the custom tailored clergy, either.

Most of the abuse of the Guru Business has come from India, or from those who have changed their names and become pseudo-Indian teachers. This is only natural, as the Indian practices are far more esoteric than those of China and Japan, reflecting the more volatile nature of the people there.

But there has been the Macrobiotic diet from Japan, with its reliance on the wondrous powers of Gen-Mai brown rice. (It is very difficult to find brown rice in Japan, the Japanese people not at all concurring in these theories.) I knew George Ohsawa, the founder, and like him, though I do not feel that he believed all he claimed. For instance, he said that he could teach anyone Japanese (a most difficult language) in four hours, a claim that was never proven. (One bright young Chinese person tried and got nowhere in four hours.) He also said he could cure leprosy by removing sugar from the diet, and claimed to have done so in a stay with Schweitzer in Africa! Such fantastic claims are easy to make if we don't have to substantiate them. What is strange is the fact that there are those who are ready to believe them. When the head of the American contingent, a kind man, died at an early age, this posed a thorny problem that was solved by saying that he would have died at an earlier age if he hadn't lived on the Macrobiotic diet!

Nonetheless, Ohsawa was a magnetic person, with some interest in Chinese Taoist beliefs (not well understood in Japan). He adapted the Yin-Yang principle to the theory of eating, and persuaded an Irish chemist to come to Japan to find out what actually happened when certain foods were ingested (perhaps indicating that Ohsawa, himself, had doubts). Results were inconclusive before the chemist went away.

Nobody would argue with the principle of simple eating, but I have seen young Americans try the extreme diet (nothing but brown rice), lose twenty or thirty pounds in a month, and become glassy-eyed and almost incoherent. So, reluctantly, we might have to conclude that such dietary fads fit into our description of the Guru business.

There have been many highly-respected teachers from the Orient who have visited this country, such as Charan Singh of the Punjab and Dr. Rammurti Mishra of Bengal, and I fail to see how they, in any way, have materially profited from their visits. It is not so much what a Master teaches that affects us as what he is! This might be a point of guidance for those caught up in the vortex of Guru claims.

Zen, by its iconoclastic nature — no worship, no footkissing, nothing but a painful facing of the self — does not lend itself to exploitation. It is a difficult discipline, concerned with ultimates, and it demands long hours of silent, painful sitting instead of metaphysical fireworks. Moreover, true Zen study requires close and continuous contact with the teacher — the Master's role cannot be delegated to others so as to spread the teaching more widely. Nevertheless, we have had the phenomena, in the West, of those who have never practised, writing books explaining the Satori experience, interpreting koans (Zen problems), introducing the meaning of Zen to eager newcomers, and forming Buddhist societies in well-meaning but misleading gestures. A great Zen teacher once asked me to write a book refuting the work of the most conspicuous of the Zen imitators, a task I quickly turned down. These writers, who often sell well (people mistake glibness for profundity) have usually read books by the respected Daisetz Suzuki (who was himself a Jodo Shinshu Buddhist, not a Zennist), and have paraphrased them into near-best sellers. Most people would prefer to read clever books ABOUT Zen rather than the few works that stem from the Zen experience itself. And for very good reason. The pseudo-works are more logical, better written, and highly conceptual, so more satisfying to the lukewarm reader, the one who is reluctant to get his own feet wet. It must be remembered that a Roshi — a true Zen Master — is a spiritual descendant of the Buddha himself, having participated in the direct transmission and not merely one who happens to be bright or number one in some group.

Two authentic Zen Masters who came to this country and stayed to offer traditional training, Roshi Shunryu Suzuki and Rinzai Master Joshu Sasaki, Roshi, cannot, by any means, be included in the Guru Parade. Roshi Suzuki, now deceased, worked quietly and without obvious reward to establish the Zen Center in San Francisco and Tassajara Monastery, near Monterey, both unusual projects at the time they were begun.

He was a lovely man, with a warm, sympathetic presence, and yet there was an element of steel in his makeup, apparent to anyone who met him. We can use more such invaders! One time, when I remarked that I had better leave Tassajara before the sun went down to begin the tortuous ride home in my old car, he merely commented that "the moon gives light, too."

My teacher, Roshi Joshu Sasaki, is a lion who gives of himself profusely. I can see no way in which he has profited by his efforts, nor does he seem interested in converting others to Buddhism. His frequent trips to Catholic monasteries and other Christian retreats, to bring the seven-day meditation known as Sesshin to the sincere seekers there, find him putting on the habit of the Order he is visiting, blending in with the background of the moment, whatever it might be. One story might illustrate this non-assertiveness, the willingness to help and to save without making any demands, except that the student try to manifest his own nature.

I had been living at Roshi's Zendo, following the life of the Monks while also working in the outside world. A young Zen student, about nineteen, had come to Roshi direct from college, and was maturing rapidly in the demanding spiritual atmosphere of the Zendo. His parents, probably regretting his defection from school, came to visit him before leaving for a foreign country to set up a library for the American government. It seemed to be a rather glamorous assignment, and one could detect that they would like their son to leave the religious life and go with them. It undoubtedly promised to be a broadening experience for a young man.

The matter was discussed around a large table, with translator, Roshi, and myself complementing the earnest parents and their son. At no time during the long interview did Roshi interfere as the parents tried to persuade the son to leave with them. He could easily have reassured them with: "Your son is a fine boy. Leave him with me a few years and you'll see great results." Roshi is not a con man, however, and he offers no easy way. Only his presence, which is dynamic, was felt during the interview, and, finally, when the parents indicated it was time to leave and looked to their son for an answer, the latter merely said: "I think I'll stay here with Roshi."

I have never heard Roshi cajole anybody; he tells it "like it is," even when this means pulling the rug out from under someone. "Strict Compassion" might be the best description of his efforts.

So there seems to be no way Roshi can personally profit by the strenuous efforts which are slowly draining his strength. (He is a strong man!) Those who want to be fooled, for their own good, and remain in the realms of illusion, should not come to such a teacher. They would be better off with one of the kindly Gurus. I have often heard Roshi say: "Outside, you are a social human being, but in here you must see with religious eyes!" The traditional Master's stick pounding the ground emphasizes such points, and it can bring terror to the faint-hearted! We are richer for such teachers; the more the better.

Have I been too harsh on the Parade of the Gurus? I hope not because I actually feel it is well worth exploitation by the many to receive the teaching — and inspiration — of the few. The 1970s were a time of spiritual renaissance in this country, and we can certainly profit by the ancient Wisdom of the East. So, welcome Guru! If you profit unduly by your missionary work, that is a matter between you and your conscience. In the meantime, I bring my palms together, bow, and welcome you with "Peace to all Beings!"

CHAPTER 3

NEW CAPITAL
OF MATERIALISM

W e arrived in the lovely mountain town of Nikko in midmorning and it was cooler than expected, due to the altitude. As always in late October, the Momiji (maple trees) were changing color, and the mountainside was breathtaking as we rode in a taxi along the winding road toward spectacular Kegon Falls. Everybody who comes to Nikko must see this waterfall.

Of the thousands of tourists on the early morning train, only I, the foreigner, seemed aware of what the name "Kegon" meant. It was simply the Japanese pronunciation of the Chinese name for a very subtle and philosophic form of Buddhism, so profound in its content that it has practically disappeared in Japan. The Japanese are not philosophers, being "feel" people, with great emotional sensitivity, rather than "think" people, depending on the intellect.

I was really looking forward to the effect of seeing Kegon Falls. The wide sweep of waterfalls in many parts of the world gives a feeling of grandeur and a sense of freedom that is very elevating to the spirit.

However, I was doomed to disappointment. Arriving at the locality, my two companions and I queued up in a long line. It was necessary to buy tickets so we could descend in a huge and crowded elevator to a promontory on which we would stand for a few minutes to enjoy the captive view, then ascend once more in the same elevator to the main level, passing incoming mobs of camera-carrying tourists, all smiling and cheerful in spite of having caught trains at Tokyo station in the pre-dawn rain at about 5:00 a.m. Everybody in Japan willingly waits in line — for taxis at a railroad station; for service on the bottom floors of the mammoth department stores where food is sold; for streetcars and buses that travel inter-city; and for almost everything else that takes place in the crowded life of this beautiful country.

Somehow, having to pay to watch a captive waterfall for a few minutes did not appeal to me, though I should have expected it. Can you imagine imprisoning the majestic Grand Canyon so one would have to buy a ticket to stand for a few minutes along its edges and dutifully photograph the awesome sight!

This minor incident seemed characteristic of what is happening in what, to me, is the most aesthetic country in the world. The forces of materialism are so rapidly overcoming the traditional character of the Japanese that a whole new generation is growing up with little sense of the beauty in Japanese life, and with a crowded suburban mentality that may doom all Japanese tradition to oblivion. Young people today see nothing strange about selling tickets to an elevator in order to descend to the Falls; it seems natural to capitalize on any situation possible and make money at every opportunity.

Another example: a young University teacher who lives near Osaka, and who was an old friend of mine, got married. As was the custom, he had an immense ceremony, complete with master-of-ceremonies, music, microphones, and professional photographers, though he probably only earns about $300 a month at his English-teaching job. (He speaks the most perfect English of anyone I know in Japan and reads Chaucer in the original.) During the day-long festivities, the bride wore four expensive costumes — and I do mean expensive! The formal kimono, with underskirts, for a wedding can easily cost $1000. (The groom, for some reason, always wears a western morning coat and striped trousers, as do the male guests!) Then there was another, less formal, kimono for the reception (bride-watching is one of the big events of the day), and, finally, a breathtaking white western wedding dress with veil, before the pretty bride changed into her smart traveling suit for the train ride to Kyushu Island, one of the customary places for young couples to go on honeymoon trips (Guam and Hawaii being two others).

Such an extravagant ceremony, with all stops pulled out, can put the poor groom into hock for ten years. (Fortunately, he doesn't have to worry about the possibility of losing his job, as employment in Japan is usually lifelong!) But no Japanese would think of opposing such an affair and saying, "Let's have a simple ceremony and spend the money on something else, or better yet, bank it." Pictures from the ceremony will fill a thick scrapbook, which all visitors will henceforth dutifully scrutinize. Since divorce is rare — and difficult — in Japan, chances of future embarrassment, because of a split-up, is relatively remote. So the grand, expensive wedding is part of the scheme of things (as it is in villages in India), one more link being forged in the rapidly-growing chain of materialism sweeping Japan.

I was not in the country for the wedding, but arrived a few months later. Promptly I was invited to take a train from Kyoto to the Osaka suburb and to spend the night at my friend's new house. Since I am very fond of him, I quickly accepted.

When we arrived at his house, having driven from the station, I was not surprised at how small it was, nor at the pre-fabricated look — Japan is very tiny, space is at a premium, and the aseptic pre-fabricated way of building has long since supplanted the older and more sturdy, more satisfying and lasting, type of construction. So Japan is turning into one monosyllabic suburb.

When we entered the house, however, I was dismayed by the drabness. Dutifully, there was one semi-Japanese room with tatami on the floor, while the rest of the furniture was strictly nondescript western. The wedding gifts, such as the ornate electric clock with statuary, had been about what one would see at any similar wedding, without any distinction or any semblance of Japanese feeling about them. I was pleased, though, to see some drawings hanging on the walls that had been made by the talented bride.

After the delicious dinner, I decided to bring out my modest wedding gift, but, by that time, I had a definite presentiment that it might not be at all appropriate. I had searched all over Kyoto for a relatively old ceremonial tea bowl, used in Cha-No-Yu, the traditional Japanese Tea Ceremony. Finding one I liked, and yet could afford, was not easy as authentic tea bowls can run into thousands of dollars. I was fortunate in finding a small, greyish one of unusual shape. It had once been broken and painstakingly patched together, making it more Shibui and respected in the eyes of old-style Japanese. It was probably because of this seemingly-damaged look that the proprietor of the store sold it to me at a reasonable price. How could he know that an ordinary gaijin (foreigner) would have a liking for things that were Wabi Sabi, austere and deceptively simple?

When my friends opened the gift box, no expression of disappointment showed in their faces — Japanese are too disciplined for that.

But the young man and I are friends, and he sometimes thinks in English. So he spoke frankly.

"What is it?" he asked.

I was surprised. "It's a Chawan (tea bowl)," I answered.

He frowned, still gazing at the antique.

"What do you use it for? It's cracked!" he remonstrated.

"You look at it," I replied, "unless you intend to have formal tea ceremony."

He shook his head, claiming to have never been at a formal Cha-No-Yu ceremony in his life except when I had trapped him into one in the beautiful Tenrikyo Kotoku Teahouse one time when he had come to visit me — much to the discomfort of his legs, not used to such squatting.

"Well, these cracks should make it more Shibui," I added hopefully, but his raised eyebrows soon stopped that line of thought.

"Where can we put it?" he finally asked in a somewhat exasperated tone, and I saw that he had me there. In the whole two-story house there was no place where the tea bowl could fit in among the doodads and gimcracks of modern Japanese life. I had to admit my gift was a total failure, and once again I had been trapped in the past of Japan and lost sight of its tawdry present. Beautiful Japan — the world's new Capital of Materialism.

This mushrooming materialism inevitably has a strange effect on the older people of the country, quite apart from the growing alcoholism and chain smoking so obvious to the observer.

Let me take one small incident in Kyoto to show this dislocation. That ancient city is covered with alleys that are not like the alleys of the West, but are really small arteries containing all kinds of shops and fruit stands. To watch kamikaze-like taxi drivers race their tiny vehicles in both directions down a thoroughfare ten feed wide, with girl students walking arm in arm, children playing in front of their houses, and delivery boys on bicycles, with tea trays balanced on their heads, pedalling delicately along, sometimes bowing to acquaintances without spilling the tea, is quite a sight. The drivers must be playing a game something like "chicken" because they tend to accelerate speed as they approach each other, and the gap between passing cabs cannot be measured in inches but in micro-millimeters. However, in my experience, nothing untoward ever happens, though Japan does have a very high accident rate.

In such narrow alleys, with shops alternately run by really pretty merchants' daughters and by old obaasan (grandmas in kimono), I used to walk home, by preference, at night. Since most shopkeepers and their families live in a room or rooms behind their shops — in which they stuff everything at night, including the inevitable motorcycle — one can buy fruit, cakes, or bread until late, there being no reason for the shops to close until the family goes to sleep. (Japan is an honest country and it is perfectly safe to leave the shops unattended. The customer will shout "Sumimasen!" when he has picked out his merchandise and is ready to pay for it.)

Walking home one evening, I decided to buy one of the large and delicious apples so plentiful in the autumn, and take it back to my temple room to peel and eat. I had often passed one grandma's little fruit stand, where her hapless young male assistant had polished the fruit till one could see a reflection in it. (The assistant was not expected to be idle during the twelve or fourteen hours at work each day, and he seemed quite used to the scoldings he frequently received.) Here I stopped and, noting that all the fruit was in baskets of four, six, or more, simply took one apple out and held it up to the light.

"How much?" I asked Obaasan.

She hesitated. Only a crazy foreigner would break up the neat packaging, and she had no idea how much one apple should sell for. Nevertheless, this is the "new" Japan, and she had to function as a cog of the Gross National Product without losing face.

"One hundred fifty yen," she called out. I was startled. That was quite expensive, and I was certainly being overcharged. Nonetheless I paid her, said, "Rest easy," (good night) and walked on.

The next morning I again passed Obaasan's fruit stand. She gave no sign of recognition, though there aren't many tall foreigners walking down her alley. I decided to make another purchase, partly to test her and partly to lay in a store for the rest of the day — visitors to the country are always very fond of Japanese fruit.

This time I picked two large apples out of the baskets, and added two packages of delicious sesame cookies. "How much?" I asked.

She slowly shook her head from side to side. Why didn't the foreigners leave the packages as they had been arranged, with nice, neat price tags on each?

"Ninety yen!" she called out resignedly. I was not surprised. If one apple costs 150 yen, it only followed that, to Obaasan in the new, commercial Japan, two apples and two packages of cookies should cost ninety yen!

Is it any wonder that Obaasan, along with practically all the young men of Japan, has become a chain smoker?

In Tokyo's famous Ginza sector, there is a high-rise building that has nothing but bars in it, bars with hostesses and bars without hostesses on every floor! Each bar has its own clients, who come there to drink after business is finished during the evening, and often to make arrangements for the not-too-subtle subsidized seduction of the available femininity working in the bar's employ. Occasionally the bar girls, or hostesses (they are not Geisha) are foreign women, preferably blond, and ads often appear in the English newspapers asking, "Do you think you can attract a man?"

Apparently the average Japanese man has little confidence in his ability to interest a woman, sans payment of some sort, and he has neither the stomach nor time for the type of dalliance so popular in Europe. If he is a prosperous businessman (and who else would be found in the bars, felt to be perfectly respectable?), he works much too hard, for excessively long hours, to bother about the leisurely approach, through flowers and other gifts, to a desirable beauty. Since he likes to drink — and much of Japan seems on its way to becoming alcoholic, not with traditional sake, but with hard whiskey — it makes sense for him to spend his money in the bars (often with credit cards), knowing some of it will be funneled to the hostess attached to him, she in turn being anxious to entice him into more frequent visits for obvious reasons. Sex paid for in one way or another seems to be the sensual epitome of life in modern Japan, and the average housewife — who is housekeeper, mother of his children, and obedient servant — usually receives her working husband back too late at night to participate in his favors. If she has his bath and a midnight snack ready for him, she has done her part.

I have a friend, a bank executive, who lives in Kamakura, almost an hour and a half by train from Tokyo. Despite the distance, he is in his office on the Ginza by 8:30 each morning, and it is a rare evening when he leaves his office, to go to a bar or a nearby MahJong club, before 10:00 p.m. (When I first met him I thought he was in his fifties, but thirty-nine turned out to be his correct age. Perhaps the rapidly-developing tic on his right cheek misled me.) I asked him when he sees his children, and he replied, "On Sundays." I reminded him that he usually plays golf on his one day of rest. (There are few golf courses in crowded Japan, and playing golf, which is extremely popular, often means going to an ingeniously-constructed driving range that holds up to 150 aficionados on several different levels.) "Well, in that case, I meet them the following Sunday," he answered, seeing nothing unusual in this perennial estrangement from his family.

I don't believe he could explain to me why he works so hard, why he forsakes the vacations due him, and why he feels such loyalty to his company, for whom he will undoubtedly labor the rest of his life, comfortable in means, with frequent use of the company credit card, but by no account rich. This last, the unbelievable loyalty, is probably a carryover from the feudal period when the subject owed everything, including his life, to his Daimyo, or Overlord — and this loyalty is repaid. It is rare for a company to dismiss an employee for any reason, choosing instead to make some face-saving excuse and quietly shuttle him to a less demanding position.

I once explained to my banker friend about the Executive Counseling agencies in America that always advise clients to be on the lookout for better positions, but he could not understand their purpose at all.

"Supposing you didn't want to work so hard?" I suggested. "Could you look around for another, less trying job? After all, you are a top executive."

He shook his head in disbelief. "Such a thing is unheard of in Japan," he explained. "This is a relatively small country, and everybody would know if I left my company. I would never find another suitable position!"

So he will continue to slowly kill himself, feeling he is enjoying his work and happy in the occasional use of the company limousine-with-chauffeur (always a black Mercedes), along with the company credit card.

When he visited me in America for two weeks, he eagerly looked around for a young woman, preferably a college girl, with whom he could form a short-term alliance. Since he admitted doing the same whenever he traveled in Japan, and was a frequent visitor to the female-stocked bars on the Ginza, I wondered whether his extramarital privilege also extended to his wife.

"Supposing, just supposing, that while you are with a woman here or in Japan, your wife should seek the company of another man — wouldn't that seem fair?" I prodded him.

He blanched. "I'd kill her!" was his only answer, and that about sums up marital responsibilities in "modern" commercial Japan. Women's Liberation will take some time to become established in this ancient country.

There is one English expression with which even non-English-speaking people in Japan are familiar — "economic animal." Businessmen and others are particularly sensitive about it, and frequently ask foreign visitors if they have heard the expression. Many times I have had to answer that I have never heard the phrase used in America, where people admire the industrious ways of the Japanese, but only in cities in other Asian nations, including Hong Kong and Singapore (which is certainly a case of the pot calling the kettle black!). Japan's presence during World War II is still vividly remembered in these places, and this, plus the obvious affluence of the numerous Japanese tourists, openly flaunted, is not calculated to endear the Japanese to other Orientals. So the Japanese man is contemptuously called "economic animal," thereby inadvertently including the scholar, the Buddhist monk, the poet, and the Japanese aesthete who steeps himself in the traditional Arts of old Japan. As I say, Japanese people are very sensitive to this expression, heard more in business centers such as Nagoya, Osaka, and Tokyo. The Japanese businessman utters "economic animal" with a laugh, but there is no humor in it.

The obvious commercialization of Religion in Japan is noteworthy, and I have had good opportunity to observe it. And yet, I can truthfully say there has been somewhat of a spiritual renaissance since the War, most easily noted in the so-called New Religions (Buddhism and Shinto, often mixed, being the traditional faiths of Japan, with Christianity clinging to a mere foothold after hundreds of years). The new religions, far from being other-worldly, usually offer counseling in everyday problems and probably serve as the psychotherapists for modern Japan.

These religions are frequently very rich, even when the majority of their adherents are ordinary working people or farmers. The fantastic organizational ability of the Japanese shines in their management, and everything is meticulously planned, nothing being left to chance. The leaders — the clergy at various levels — know well what the Japanese character demands, and they expeditiously shape their Religion to these needs, often borrowing from Buddhism or Christianity on the way and ingeniously reshaping the borrowed material. And so the contributions pour in, usually in small denominations, such as five or ten yen.

Buddhism has long been the dominant religion in Japan, and many adherents of the New Religions also consider themselves Buddhists. It would be hard to overestimate the influence Buddhism has had on the Japanese Culture and Customs, particularly the influence of Zen. The Theatre, Garden, Flower Arrangement, Tea Ceremony, Dance and Architecture all have been Zen-influenced, and it would not be an exaggeration to say the attitudes and lifestyle of all Japanese owe something to Zen training.

And yet, Zen seems to be in a long, slow decline in Japan, fighting dual adversaries: the New Religions and the Materialistic attitude that is taking people away from any spiritual leaning and making Affluence the new God. Ever since Government subsidy has been withdrawn from the Zen temples, they have been hard put to stay afloat. The result? When one goes to see the beautiful stone garden at Ryoanji, or the forty-nine kinds of moss at Saiho-ji (my favorite temple, popularly known as "Kokadera"), one buys tickets at an office, queuing up in long lines intent on quick glimpses of these historic sites. And does one see monks meditating there? Of course not — the only personnel apparent are the ticket takers.

When I traveled deep into the mountains to visit Eihei-ji, the great Zen Master Dogen's own temple, I was dismayed to find monks who spend their entire days greeting guests, making change, and carrying out all the financial transactions of a hostel. Of course, there are monks who sweep the guest rooms and do other domestic tasks. Since as many as 300 overnight guests come at one time, all the problems of a hotel — and financial dealings, for it is not free — descend upon the home-leavers, who presumably came there to pursue enlightenment. Movies about Zen were shown, and my friend and I seem to have been the only guests who came there to practise Zazen. The morning service was colorful and full-blown, with stunning trappings designed to impress the laity — resembling more the workings of the Catholic Church than the understated instructions of the Founder, Dogen. I realize the sect is making its stand now against inroads of the New Religions and the New Affluence, and a little Madison Avenue is perhaps understandable. The trouble is, such compromise with principle usually results in the Means becoming the End, and then the ancient Hierarchy becomes just one more business institution competing in the fevered Market Place.

The emphasis on selling tickets, even in the religious Shrines, is so widespread that any Japanese would be astonished if a visitor would find anything unusual about the practice. And yet, if one goes to Florence, Italy, does he buy a ticket if he wants to pray in the Cathedral and watch the Michelangelo "Pieta" in the fading twilight? Is there a fence around the huge statue of David, and does one enter an elevator to descend to a level where he may briefly view it? Hardly. It is the legacy of Florence to the world, and one may view it at leisure without ringing the cash register.

This avarice, this willingness to work unconscionably long hours in the name of national prosperity, and this desire for artificial things (kaimono — things to buy) is so great that it may change the character of the ancient nation. Rows of discount appliance stores, selling thousands of color television sets, stay in the memory of the visitor along with the historic cultural landmarks. The world may soon think of Japanese solely in terms of the Toyota and the supertanker, rather than in the image of a leisurely life of grace and beauty. Then the Japanese will no longer be skilled and painstaking craftsmen, but all will be mechanics. The traditional reserve and understatement of the people seem doomed to perish in the face of brash salesmanship. Perhaps Japan is slowly losing its soul.

A recent memory of Tokyo, trivial in itself, may highlight the dichotomies of prosperous new Japan. In mid-afternoon at a neighborhood tea room, one sees obaasan and ojiisan (grandma and grandpa) sitting at a small table, eating chocolate parfait and sipping the delicious (and expensive!) coffee with obvious relish. Grandma is wearing traditional kimono, while Grandpa is sporting a new Pierre Cardin tie and imported Italian shoes. The afternoon wears on, and they are enjoying themselves — then suddenly, having looked at expensive wristwatches, they both jump to their feet and rush to the door. Not wishing to be late for dinner, they hail a passing taxicab, easy to find in crowded Tokyo. Did you perhaps expect them to walk home?

To those who found some beauty in the older ways, this is dismaying. But in this enlightened century of science, it is happening all over the world. It is just that the contrast is so marked in Japan, where delicacy was once a way of life.

CHAPTER 4

Ramana Maharshi — photograph from *The Mountain Path*

The Three-Step Religions:

BUDDHISM AND YOGA

A traveling Vedanta monk once said to me: "Do good, be good — that is the essence of all Religion."

This, of course, is an oversimplification. Morality is a very necessary preliminary to true Religion, but it has been likened to the steps leading to a bridge. While the steps are essential, it is the bridge, after all, that carries one across.

In the West we have come to look on Religious thinking as simply a call to Higher Morality: be "good" and your reward will be Heaven, be "bad" and you will go to Hell. The preacher, in his Sunday sermon, is against "sin," though sin is often a matter of geography. Suffice it to say, we should obey the commandments or the precepts; that is about all he can expect from us. If we are devout, we may wish to follow certain established ritual, which will certainly impress our subconscious. If not, we can rest secure in anticipation of a future life not too unpleasant, as we feel we have been pretty good in our present life — by and large.

There are two three-step Religions that want adherents to go far beyond this simple formula, however, and have as their aim the actual manifestation of Divinity in the form of Enlightenment or True Realization. They are Yoga and Buddhism.

Of course, Yoga (true Yoga, not what has generally been sold in the West) is a science. Certain causes will, inevitably, produce certain effects. But it is also a Religion, if we define Religion as "Concern with Ultimates," though it is not theistically inclined.

The great Patanjali is generally thought of as the "Father" of Yoga, though he was not its founder — Yoga antedates any sort of history, written or remembered. His "Yoga Sutras" are the Bible of Yoga, and in them he has organized this practice, belief, or Religion (take your pick) into three parts, making up the Kingly Yoga called Raja. These three parts are divided into eight steps, which cover about all the known practices of Indian Yoga. The three parts are:

1) The Preliminary-Moral: the two prerequisites for successful Yogic practice are YAMA and NIYAMA, which have to do with such matters as conduct, attitude, and inquiry.

2) The Outer-Physical Disciplines, which are three: ASANA (posture, sometimes thought of as "exercise" in the West), PRANAYAMA (the Science of Prana, all energy — often associated with the breath), and PRATYAHARA (withdrawal of the senses from their fields of action; transmutation of psychic energy).

3) The Superconscious State: CONCENTRATION, MEDITATION (Dhyana), and SAMADHI.

One practising Yoga, with Ultimate Union as his goal (the true purpose of Yoga, from which we get our word "yoke," meaning "to bind together"), must certainly start with the idea of non-injury to all beings, physical, psychological, and any other kind. This, of course, implies truthfulness, and all other such standards of conduct, not so much for purely moral reasons as for the effect such actions have on the mental processes. Habit energies that are formed by negative actions lead us more deeply into the realms of illusion, which is bondage, and this is what we are struggling against. From darkness into light is our aim, so purification of the nervous system is a must. Harmful actions, mental or physical, which leave their stain on the mind (and the psyche), must be dispensed with, for our own good.

There is no promise of a lasting "Heaven" in Yoga. We expect to come back to this suffering life again and again until, finally, some Wisdom dawns and we begin to follow the way that will grant us Release. And the way to this Release involves a retracing of the steps we have taken. The great Sage, Ramana Maharshi, advised: "Go back the way you came!" When causes are annulled, the effects will drop away of themselves. We are, literally, the habit energies and tendencies ("vashanas" and "samskaras" in Sanskrit) that we have built up through many lives, says Yoga, and by dimming and erasing these, we nullify the effects that inevitably flow from them. If we want to remake the world, we remake ourselves. Yoga leads to Vairagya, which is detachment and dispassion. Relative desirelessness is a necessary end, as it

40

is desire that sets in motion the chain of circumstances leading to the making of the mental habit patterns, the vashanas. Indeed, Patanjali defines Yoga as "the restriction of mental modifications," and this must be understood in the sense of not-making new habit patterns, the all-powerful vashanas.

It can be easily seen why there is no Yoga Church. The dogma, ritual, and priestcraft so necessary to Christianity have no place in Yoga. There is only the Teacher, who passes on what he has realized (in truth, points the way to follow in his footsteps). Church Religions are dual in nature — the worshipper and the worshipped, the clergy and the laity — while the Science of union deals with One Force only (this despite the fact that the Samkya Philosophy usually associated with Yoga starts from a limited dual premise). Union is Union; there are not two in such Union.

Any sectarianism or denominational narrowness would be impossible in this three-tier Yoga Religion. Anyone can be a Yogi; anyone can attain Union. In a sense, there have been Yogis in every Religion, very often looked down upon or persecuted as being roadblocks in the business of Church Religion. Hence, many of the martyrs of all faiths.

Practically all the great teachers I have met in the world were beyond any sectarian feeling, often having no formal Religion of their own. Mankind is their Religion; all beings are themselves. This represents a high level of Yoga, implying fulfillment of the three steps, the Moral, the Outer-Physical, and the Inner leading to Superconsciousness. One who has mastered these steps is on his way to being a god, and as such, is the greatest influence mankind can know. The Saint is, by definition, good. The Sage goes far beyond this and represents the top level in the three-stage development of Yoga.

There are many types of Buddhism in the world, each of which exists at several levels. The Buddha's original Enlightenment Experience, which he sought to pass along, was far deeper than most want to go. (The average person is not searching for the Ultimate Truth of Being, but for a comfortable, secure life.) Accordingly, through his forty-nine year ministry after his Enlightenment, during which he set in motion his marvelously thorough teaching, the Buddha generally dealt with aspects of Truth rather than the Whole, an accommodation meant to bring along the members of the

Sangha (Buddhist Community) bit by bit until they were ready to receive — and experience — the Ultimate Teaching. True Buddhist teaching is wonderfully complete. What is lacking is not in the teaching, but in the ability of followers to assimilate it.

So the Buddhism we find today in the world usually deviates greatly from the Master's teaching. The Buddhism of Japan has been mixed with Shinto, and colored by the characteristics of the Japanese people, which are almost diametrically opposed to those of Buddha's own Indian people. The Japanese and Chinese do not have the metaphysical leanings of the Indian people, the genius that led to the Upanishads, the Bhagavaad Gita, the Yoga Sutras of Patanjali, and the six involved Darshanas (or Philosophical Systems) of India. A Ramakrishna, a Yogi Vasistha, a Ramana Maharshi, or a poet-devotee such as Kabir, would be unthinkable in Eastern Asia, where the Devotional aspects do not have the appeal we find in India.

On the other hand, the Chinese and Japanese have a hardworking practicality, with great vitality, that has made possible Taoism and Zen Buddhism, neither at all Indian in makeup. In Japan we have the largest sect, Jodo Shinshu, with its total dependence on "The Other Power," complete surrender to the Buddha of Infinite Light, who will take the true believer to the Western Paradise, where conditions for reaching Enlightenment will be more favorable than on this planet's suffering premises. Jodo is a beautiful belief, and very effective, with its simple formula of constant repetition of the "Hail to the Buddha of Infinite Light" (Namu Amida Butsu), spoken from a heart emptied of all but devotion. Yet this is the direct opposite of the Buddhism taught by the Buddha. He said, "Work Out Your Own Salvation!" and "Believe Only Your Own Experience." "Be a Lamp Unto Yourselves" meant no reliance on any Other, no matter how exalted. This is not egocentric; in Buddhism there truly is no Other.

And so, the Buddhism we find in Taiwan, in China, in Japan, and in Tibet, differs greatly from the Master's teaching. Probably only Sri Lanka and Burma, with possibly a few other isolated places, still preserve the "pessimistic" search for Nirvana (meaning "Extinction," but not in the ordinary sense) that was the basis of the Buddha's Way.

Gautama Buddha pointed to three Universals where beings are concerned: Impermanence (Anicca), Suffering (Dukkha), and No-Soul No-Entity (An-Atman). The first two are easy for anyone to understand, for no thinking person will gainsay Impermanence and Suffering, evidence of which is constantly around us. The An-Atman is more difficult to grasp. Without knowing the meaning of "Dependent Origination," one cannot understand that all things — and individual beings — stand in relationship to each other. Buddhism expresses this as "That arising, this arises." All is relative, even consciousness, and depends on conditions. This effectively does away with any "Absolute." In Buddhism there is no Transcendental Buddha.

The An-Atman teaching is a Truth that belies what we have learned in the other Religions, theistically inclined, where we have been comforted in the thought that we had "an immortal soul," which could be saved by "being good." Buddhism does away with the idea of "Divine Grace," dealing always in cause and effect; there is no result without something putting it into motion. Thus, in Buddhism, the idea of a Creator God would, of necessity, call for a previous cause to account for the Deity. Consequently, in Buddhism, we must think of Time as circular rather than extending from here to there, with beginning and end.

The Buddha is usually referred to as "The Compassionate Buddha," and so he concentrated on pointing out the way to end Suffering. This Suffering is not merely the "pain" in the pleasure-pain syndrome; the Buddha said that, in the long run, pleasure, too, is Suffering. Suffering really means the pain of being separated from our True Identity; and Individualism, which we prize so much, is the best example of this separation. So he taught the "Four Noble Truths," which had to do with the Origin of Suffering and the Way to follow the Road to the Extinction of Suffering. The Buddha had no theories and no speculative philosophy. From his Great Enlightenment he taught the steps to end Suffering in an entirely pragmatic manner, ending it not only for this lifetime but for all time to come.

Impermanence, Suffering, and No-Soul No-Entity are, of course, interrelated. In our own everyday lives, our inability to accept impermanence — because things are going well now, we assume they always will; and because our young love is beautiful, we feel she will always be — brings suffering, and our identification with an "I" when truly there is no abiding "I" also makes for immeasurable suffering.

The purpose of this chapter, however, is not to get into the Noble Truths the Buddha taught, or his Eightfold Path, but to point out why, like Yoga, Buddhism is a three-tiered Religion, going two steps beyond most Religions. The Buddha was not interested in teaching his followers how to be good and go to Heaven. He admitted there are Heavens — many of them — but said life there, too, is impermanent and eventually one will fall to earth again "like a spent arrow," having made no progress at all toward a permanent and abiding Salvation.

The three steps of Buddhism might be called: 1) SILA (Conduct-Morality), 2) DHYANA-SAMADHI (Meditation carried to the deepest level), and 3) PRAJNA (The Practice of Wisdom). The first, so wonderfully stated in the Buddha's dynamic "Dhammapada," is the moral teaching of all Religions. He spoke with great care and thoroughness, using constant repetition to drive home the necessity of proper conduct, mental and physical, as the prerequisite for traveling the Road to Enlightenment — much as in Raja Yoga.

The Buddha told his followers not to dispute with, nor make uncomfortable, those who were not ready to understand. And he said it was useless to discuss Buddhism at any length with one who was not himself meditating. The intellect simply cannot handle the realization; one must actually experience it in the Body-Mind continuum we refer to as "ourselves." And so the Chinese say: "You cannot appease your hunger by reading a menu." Only those meditating and practising the Way can advance along the path of Dhyana (Meditation) to Samadhi, the constant Truth-Awareness that Zen adepts refer to as "Twenty-Four-Hour Zen." This second step takes us, without the physical disciplines that are a preliminary to it in Yoga, to the same level Patanjali described as the culmination of Raja Yoga. In Buddhism there is yet another step, perhaps unique in the history of Religious teaching.

This is the practice of Prajna (Wisdom). The great Sixth Patriarch of Zen, Hui Neng, was untutored and illiterate throughout his life, yet all subsequent Zen schools descend directly from him. Before he even shaved his head to become a monk, he had demonstrated the function of Prajna Wisdom

44

very clearly. When he had been a simple woodcutter, he one day heard a recitation of the "Diamond Sutra," a Buddhist Scripture, and upon hearing the single line, "The Mind (HSIN in Chinese, meaning Heart-Mind-Spirit) that abides No-where," he realized Enlightenment. This is a perfect example of the Prajna Wisdom shining forth by its own light (Zen uses the expression, "Show Me Your Face Before You Were Born!") — not blocked by conceptual thinking, sentiment, or illusion of any kind. I don't want to go into a discussion of the Alaya Vijnana, the Eighth Consciousness (the Great Storehouse), but it is a shining example of the Mirror Brightness manifesting far beyond the power of any individual intellect to do so. There have been many occasions in Zen history when a carelessly thrown tile striking bamboo, or the sudden sound of the bottom dropping out of a water cask, have brought this shining Wisdom to the surface and enabled the monk (or layman) to experience the most profound Enlightenment. We are told of the three weeks of ecstasy experienced by Shakyamuni (the Buddha) himself when, after emerging from four levels of Meditation, he saw the Morning Star and experienced his Complete Enlightenment. Here we have the Prajna Wisdom unblocked, shining forth by its own light and cognized as Bliss. All Yoga and Buddhist Masters have stressed that Bliss is man's essential nature.

So the third step, the manifesting of the Prajna function — which Hui Neng stressed was as important as the practise of Dhyana-Samadhi, the second step — is unique in Buddhism. When there is unconditioned reflex action and reaction, and when we speak, sleep, eat, and eliminate spontaneously, without hangup, we are demonstrating the way of "The True Man of No Title," as Zen Master Rinzai called him. This is Prajna Wisdom, and the functioning of it is the beginning of True Life. Perhaps this is the meaning of the incident where the Buddha held up a flower, and only Maha Kasyapa of all those in the great assembly understood the meaning of the gesture. The others were lost in the object, the flower, and so the victims of ratiocination; only Great Kasyapa realized "That" which held up the flower, and this was the functioning of the Prajna Wisdom.

So, in Spiritual Practice, it depends on just how far we want to go. If we are concerned with simple Theological Salvation, most any Religion will give it to us, along with a measure of contentment. But if we truly want to experience Ultimates, I believe we will have to tread one of the Paths of Yoga or the Way of Buddhism to reach where we are going. And this is not for the timid or the weak.

CHAPTER 5

RANDOM NOTES

T he worlds are built by ourselves, and so we cannot escape from them. The trick is to find the Truth in each step of the way, to penetrate to the heart. We find ourselves, our happiness, and our God in our relationships with others — we find God in the hearts of men. And we come to know that each is singing the Glory of Creation.

Nothing happens without cause. In each moment we must speak or act in such a way that the effect will be desirable. The potential must be the seed of the fruitful. So we take care!

The unreal mind searches for objects. The mind resting-in-itself (complete subjectivity) is Reality.

Your Spiritual I.Q. is the degree to which you identify with Reality. It has nothing to do with intellectual prowess.

The true teacher is a servant of his pupils.

Zen Taoism?

It is said of Zen that Indian Buddhism was the Father and Chinese Taoism the Mother — and that the child much more resembles the Mother than the Father!

This is true. Indian Buddhism is life-negating, while Taoism and Zen strive to affirm. In Buddha's time, those who joined the Buddhist Community (Sangha) became monks or nuns. One did not pursue the worldly life and go to church on Sunday. Those who lived monastically and practised the teachings faithfully treated the World as a forest ablaze — a place to be gotten out of. Frequent meditation on corpses and the pus, phlegm, and excrement of the human body created a detachment from Life and a loathing of the living-suffering-dying program of Life. Nirvana was a condition beyond individuality, where Life was not composed of separate entities. The idea, not different from that expressed in the Upanishads, was to "get off the wheel of Life and Death" and recapture the Bliss of Nirvana. The word "Nirvana" means "extinction," a wiping out of Life as we know it, and that is, of course, Life-negating.

On the other hand, Taoism and Zen have taught that the Great Meaning must be found in the midst of the Vale of Tears. Without escaping misery and without leaving this

impermanent Life, we are to realize our Salvation, our Nirvana, in the middle of the disappointment, the pain and the insecurity. We do not leave — we stay in the burning forest to help all other beings escape or help to make their lot more bearable. In Buddhist terms we "make a raft of ourselves" to ferry all others across suffering Samsara to the Promised Land beyond. This is not Life-negating. We find real Meaning in the absurd suffering that is the lot of all born into this fragmented Life, and it brings beauty to us, not disgust. "Every Day is a Good Day!" says the Zen Master while viewing tragedy all around him.

So we could easily call it "Zen Taoism" instead of "Zen Buddhism." The great Masters of the Golden Age of Zen in China (that ended in the T'ang Dynasty) used Taoist terminology in their sermons and usually referred to "Reality" as the Tao. Zen adepts were even responsible, at one point in history, for the renaissance of Taoism. Buddhism came from India, but it wedded with Taoism and found a national character in China uniquely suited to the offspring, Zen. This is symbolized by the fact that the First Zen Patriarch was Bodhidharma, who came from India but found his disciples and successors in China.

Unlike the other-worldly transcendent quality of Indian practice, Chinese and Japanese Zen deal in "Nowness!" Awareness of the present, without judgment or classification of same, is the absolute essential. The mind is likened to an ox that strays toward other pastures, and we yank it back over and over again. When thoughts stray, as they will, we do not follow them. When there is memory or daydream, we simply remain detached from them. While fully aware, the mind cannot be without thoughts, but they are not "our" thoughts. They come and they go and we remain untouched, deep in ourselves. When the Zen Master gives a shout, he is really shouting, "Now!" One Zen teacher, asked to write something profound, made the character for "attention" three times. Attention! Attention! Attention!

During the time of Hui Neng, the Sixth Patriarch, his rival, Shen-Hsiu, taught a meditation much like the Dhyana practice of India, holding on to one thought so the mind could become one-pointed. This teaching, with Purity as the aim, was the characteristic of the Northern School of Ch'an (Chinese Zen), but that School did not flourish and, in time, died out. Such

quietism and search for Purity — the "wiping of the mirror" to keep the dust away — was not compatible with the vitality and character of the Chinese people. The Southern School's explosive "Instant Enlightenment," not arriving gradually as we quietly purify, but bursting on the scene from our Prajna Wisdom, had more appeal. Perhaps it was the personality of Hui Neng himself that tipped the scales to the Southern School, for both methods are valid. The dynamic function of the Prajna Wisdom appealed to the Chinese, while the quiet Life-negating Dhyana (still meditation) was more in the nature of the Indian people.

Chinese and Japanese Zen actually wandered far afield from the Indian beginning, as did all Mahayana Buddhism. It is interesting, however, that Soto Zen, as taught by the great Dogen in Japan, did bring back an element of the original quietism. Emphasize the dynamism of function, as symbolized by the shouts and beatings of the great Masters; hence the question, "Should we call it 'Zen Taoism'?"

THERE IS RELIGION,
THERE ARE NO RELIGIONS.
THERE IS BEING,
THERE ARE NO BEINGS.
THERE ARE WORDS,
BUT NO ONE IS SPEAKING.
(there is nonsense, and maybe this is it.)

There are so many contradictions between religions and philosophies, but they occur at the oral level. When we try to explain in words, there is only Religion. This one Religion is no "religion." Truth is not in words; it is lived. Religion brings with it an overwhelming feeling of Gratitude and Compassion. In truth, there is nothing but Religion, call it what we may.

53

Confucius spoke of "JEN," human-heartedness, and other Chinese Sages pointed to "TEH," the power of an inner sincerity. These are only approximate translations. They lead us to feel that the Superior Man would combine a deep sincerity with compassion for others and the ability to empathize with them.

Primitive man lived close to and in awe of his origins. "Civilized" man has become alienated from them and drifts without roots. It is said that science has progressed to a point where a man may soon be able to spend his entire life in a 100-story building without ever stepping outside! A telephone call to the market on the thirtieth floor will procure groceries, and a coin in a special slot will bring a movie into the living room. It will be easy for the government to keep track of each citizen. And of course, inhabitants will be able to watch the snow on television. Man will finally have succeeded in imprisoning himself.

CHAPTER 6

THE GROWTH
OF CERTAINTY

"L"ead me from the Unreal to the Real."

This is the great Vedantic prayer that represents the height of Spirituality. In the realm of illusion we inevitably find misery, we are bound and unable to exist in Freedom. Sometimes the chains by which we are bound are golden — we are wealthy, we have health and pleasurable circumstances, and we feel smug in our existential situations — but this is all temporary. There is no contract with Divinity that such pleasant conditions will continue, and if we are at all sensitive, we are only too aware that there is untold suffering all around us. So a sudden death or tragedy may take away the ones we love most, a change of fortune may impoverish us, or unjust accusations may destroy our good name and reputation. Truly, a shift in the wind can take us from the heights to the depths without warning. It is for this reason that the Chinese Sage says: "Go to your triumph like a funeral." Few are this wise, however.

What is the answer? What defense do we have? Spiritually, the answer is to identify with the Real, which is lasting, and be indifferent, though not callous, to what is temporary and passing, however pleasurable, knowing too well how often pleasure is followed by pain.

What do we mean by the "Real"? That which is permanent, that which is not phenomenal and subject to change. In Indian Philosophy, the Real is identified negatively as "Neti Neti" — "Not this, not that." What can be apprehended by the senses is changeable, in a constant state of flux (though, truthfully, it is a symbol of the Reality underlying all phenomena). What is multiple is always in a state of transition, and to tie our hopes to it is to certainly end in disillusion. This very act of ascribing Reality to what is essentially only flux is the cause by which we create our own misery.

In truth, our "own" bodies change constantly, from fingernails to hair to beard to waste products, so that, physically, we are never the same person we were yesterday.

And do we know we will still be alive tomorrow? Each man lives as though he is immortal, while knowing full well he will inevitably die. To be smug and satisfied in this condition hardly seems wise. We can attempt to pass our time pleasurably in entertainment, trying the impossible task of cultivating pleasure while doing away with pain. Or we can clearly see the whole picture and determine to identify with a Permanence that is not subject to circumstances — this chance we have. When we determine, usually after severe suffering, to take the Eternal Road and to dedicate ourselves to realizing the Lasting, whether we call it God, Tao, Buddha, Allah, or whatever, we have, in Buddhist terminology, "entered the stream." We have turned 180 degrees from mere sense enjoyment and begun to tread the Way that will, inevitably, take us to the complete fulfillment of Spiritual Realization. This is the true Spiritual Path, and the starting point of Spirituality is usually the terrible sense of impermanence.

Many equate Spirituality with the vague and ephemeral, with a wishy-washy do-good attitude. Nothing could be farther from the truth. True Sages — and most Saints — have been vigorous and purposeful, possessed of an inner Certainty that gave a strong Center to their lives and attracted others less firmly grounded. The Spiritual task of finding Reality — really manifesting Reality — can be long and hard, but it is, in the end, the only rewarding one. There is no true contentment without it, no matter how smug we may temporarily feel in our own little niche. This Spiritual Path starts with Repentance and determination to renounce inwardly what is not Real, and it does not mean a change in the outer circumstances of our life. If it comes about through some overwhelming and unexplainable spiritual happening, as it sometimes does, well and good. A Saul of Tarsus on the road, overcome by a sudden vision of Jesus, will never forget it, and his future life will always head in the direction of Reality. This type of incident is comparatively rare, however. Most of us came to the Spiritual Path through grief. Something led us to a feeling of futility. Like a rat on a treadmill, we have followed the way of others, striving for a little security and a little pleasure, and suddenly it strikes us and, in dismay, we begin to search for something lasting, something on which we can depend. And this search is always outer. We read books, look to teachers, and travel, always with the idea that something will be added to us that will make the difference — this despite the fact that we have been told, "The Kingdom of Heaven is within," that basically, we lack nothing and are all Buddhas. I overheard an Indian teacher, when he was being profusely thanked by a disciple, disclaim the credit, saying, "I can only give you what is already yours!" So the task resolves itself into a struggle to realize ourselves, truly to be what we already basically are, and to develop our own inner treasure. The great teacher will always throw us back on ourselves, for the answer we find for ourselves is the only one that counts. And this answer will never be verbal or intellectual. God, or Reality, is not an object, something that can be defined. There is no mathematical formula involved, no sudden discovery of a hidden word or idea. The Zen teacher cautions that "the last thing a Zen student should prize is understanding." Understanding is not the way; explanation is not the aid. Somewhere deep inside we know. It is not that we must uncover light; we are the light, and it is not objectified. As we progress along the Spiritual way, the path to Manifestation of Reality, there will be a growth of something within, impossible to describe. I call it "The Growth of Certainty."

There is a religious consciousness within each of us, and it slowly matures in spite of everything unless we dull it with drugs, whiskey, hedonistic practices, or other narcotic means, such as endless meaningless diversion. No matter how superficially we live — and Lord knows, we wallow in superficiality and the provincial, afraid to take the chance of new discovery — this Spiritual Consciousness ripens and, one day, there will be fruits. We can help it to ripen, as we can water and fertilize a tree, but it can only grow because it is already present. It is present in the sinner, the drunk, the murderer, and later it will come to fruition; we can follow a path that will stimulate its growth.

The Buddha said that all suffering is the result of Greed, Anger, and Delusion. To be separated from our true Identity is to suffer, and not to recognize all things or relationships as impermanent is to be overwhelmed with suffering. To want and not to get is to suffer, and to obtain what we want and then jealously worry that it will be taken away, that, too, is to suffer. And to feel that there is a permanent entity called "I," separate from all other "I's," is to insure that there will be the greatest suffering.

First, let us examine the "permanent I."

When man dies, his body is usually buried and eaten by worms. These worms, in turn, are consumed by hungry birds. The dead birds' bodies decompose and become the earth, and from this earth grows the tree. Eventually the tree produces fruit, and this fruit is eaten by man. Soon the man dies and is eaten by worms, and the cycle has started again. Now at exactly what point did the man cease to be man and become worm; how did the "I" of the worm cease and meld into the "I" of the bird? Leaving aside the insatiable ego, which claims to be unique and undying, what can we say about this cycle except to say, "There is a Life Force continually manifesting."? This Force, this Energy, goes on, never diminishing, but the form it takes is constantly changing. So should we identify with the form, or with the Life Force itself? Should we come and go with the rapidly-changing clouds, or should we place ourselves in the position of Sky — deep, blue, endless, and fundamentally void, meaning without aspect? Where there is aspect, there is change. A God who is "Good," "Just," "Loving," and other descriptors would not be a permanent God because such qualities are relative. "Good" is only good in relation to "Bad." From the Absolute standpoint, there can be no "Good" or "Bad." And so we come to "Neti Neti" — "Not this, not that." Only through negation can we indicate Reality. It is for this reason that, though ordinary thinking may be designated as "either-or," Buddhism is the way of "neither-nor." One form of Buddhism, Kegon in Japanese, attempts to reach Reality through a series of over a hundred negations — and the last of these is the Negation of Negation. THAT which can be named is not the true THAT. "I AM THAT I AM" is a perfect description of the aspectless Reality, as long as we remember this "AM" is not the opposite of "Am Not," not "Being" as opposed to "Non-Being." It is difficult to push the mind to such overwhelming conclusions, and only through proper meditation do we find that such Realization comes naturally, without pushing. And then the true teacher asks, "What is there to Realize?" to cut off any attachment in that direction. A great teacher is like one who stands over us as we hang desperately from the cliff, treading on our fingers until, in pain and desperation, we have to let go. What is this "letting go"? It is giving up the small identity with which we have saddled ourselves, the personality through which the Life Force is temporarily manifesting. Those who practise the Spiritual Way often have experiences where the personality is completely out of the picture. There is a Knowing, but no one who is doing the Knowing. Then we snap back to the habitual, regain our habit energies, and reassume our comfortable identity. And seemingly all contact with Truth is then lost again.

Early on the Spiritual Path, stimulated by meditation and Spiritual practices, we have many psychic experiences. These encourage us. Occasionally we have a dream that is too vivid to be a dream, and we realize that it was an actual experience that does not leave us when we awaken. As time goes on, however, the mind purifies and we have fewer and fewer of these psychic happenings. Instead, there is something firm that manifests from the center of our Being, the Growth of Certainty. It can never be called "an experience" in the phenomenal sense. There is nothing on which the intellect can lay hold. And it is this very Certainty which begins to guide us. We are surprised to hear the words that come spontaneously from our mouths. If we teach, we know without conjecture what others need. There is no pondering, no indecision — there is a Knowing that derives from the Growth of Certainty. This is the beginning of the Impersonal Life, and it can never be understood by those who do not experience it.

Only the one who is called to it will find this Growth of Certainty, and all others will enjoy the world in their own way, laughing and crying by turns, with the sum total really "signifying nothing." We propagate and we die; this is the life cycle we know. Every Sage has said that this is suffering. We suffer from pain, and we suffer from pleasure. And every day we see unbelievable suffering in the world around us, though we may not admit it.

So perhaps we turn to Spiritual practice in a half-hearted way. If we make Meditation and Spiritual Practice just one more activity sandwiched in between the movies, television, lectures, and whatever others we do, then our efforts are doomed to failure. Meditation is not a diversion; amusement is not the goal. If one is too trivial to aim at Ultimates, then why bother with Spiritual Practice? Acclaim is no measure of Spiritual Depth, and ease and munificence are not the true results of practice. If there is not something crying out for a "Growth of Certainty," something puzzled by incomprehensible life and death, then why not stay on the superficial level and forego Spiritual Practice? Of course, there is always the possibility that such practice, even though sporadic, will cause a spark and gradually deepen the original aim. In fact, if the sporadic practice is continued, such result seems inevitable. We will all experience this Growth of Certainty one day.

CHAPTER 7

Japanese Sumi Painting

CERTAINTY THROUGH DEVOTION

The Way of Devotion

Devotion cultures the heart. When adoration is not selfishly demanding a return, there is a yearning toward something greater than ourselves. We lose ourselves in the immensity of the Beloved; we are nothing and thus become everything.

This is Indian Bhakti and the Lover-Beloved relationship of the Sufi poet. Naturally, it is dualistic in the beginning. We are separated, however little, from the Object of Devotion, and the true Bhakti prays to his Beloved that this separation may continue so that the ecstasy of adoration will not be lost. Unlike the follower of the Path of Knowledge, the Bhakti delights in the separateness — there will be no merging with Reality, so the identity of the lover is not lost. And yet, is this not the "self-naughting" Christian Monastics have spoken of? Is this not the Realizing of God in the true Hassidic fashion, and in the realizing, do "we" not disappear? When the cheeks are washed by involuntary tears of gratitude, a thankfulness for Being, do we not attain heights no self-striving can realize? In the simple "Namu Amida Butsu" of the Japanese Jodo Shinshu devotee, is there not a faith and a devotion that removes regard for "my" power and that places us in the position of utter dependence on the Other, saying simply "Thy Will Be Done"? Such surrender is the hottest purifying flame, and from it also comes a Certainty.

I want to tell a little about two incidents that happened to me personally. In the summer of 1971 I was staying at a Ramakrishna Vedanta Ashram near Los Angeles, recharging batteries so to speak. Having promised to give several Sunday talks there, I was spending time in Meditation, watering the huge lawns, and helping wash dishes after meals. The beauty and quiet of the place lent themselves to contemplation, and since the Ashram was situated in the foothills, the oppressive summer heat was apparent only at midday. But this idyllic situation was clouded by an antagonism that evinced itself almost from the moment I arrived. An Indian woman living on the Ashram grounds with her children took an immediate dislike to me. I, personally, admired her singing (in the true tradition of Indian Kirtan) and saw no reason for difficulty between us, but there it was. When I greeted her, she did not answer. At the dinner table there were many unpleasant comments sent my way. I realized she had been the victim of an auto accident in recent years — with a serious head injury — and did all in my power not to respond in kind, but to no avail. There was great unpleasantness, and it was felt by all.

So heavy was the weight of this antagonism that I began to seriously wonder whether I should leave the Ashram so as to spare others the unpleasantness. It did not seem that there was anything I could do to alleviate the situation.

This Ashram's spiritual practice is Devotion to Divine Mother. Many of the devotees who live there claim to have had strong experiences with Holy Mother, and others eagerly await the day when they, too, will feel the Divine Presence. Do not think of imagination or self-hypnosis. Those who have to have a "rational" explanation for every event will never know such experiences and never know the contentment that such devotion can bring. They are doomed to wander in the nether world bounded by their own narrow intellects. In any event, the morning and afternoon services are devoted to washing the feet of the Deity and other such practices, along with meditation and chanting. On Saturday nights there is Kirtan (Indian songfest), led by my lady antagonist, and a wonderful feeling is generated singing the devotional songs as we sit before the huge fireplace.

Certainly, with a background of Zen Buddhist practice, such Bhakti is not my way. And yet, I could not help but feel the strong vibrations of the Ashram and enjoyed the services and meditation. Finally, in despair over the deteriorating personal situation, I decided to put Holy Mother to the test.

During the afternoon service I prayed very hard, a departure from my usual way where prayer is simply a giving of thanks. "Holy Mother," I beseeched, "I don't know how you can do it, but please heal this awful breech that has developed. I ask it, not for my sake, but for the benefit of all." Then after Service, we went to dinner as usual, washed the dishes, and I slowly walked down the road, under the many stars, to the guest home where I slept.

No sooner had I entered the door than the phone began to ring. I picked it up and was surprised to hear the distraught voice of the Indian lady. She said she had tried the phones of all the other cottages on the grounds, and none had answered — very strange in itself. As a last resort, she appealed to me. Something had happened to her dog and she was frantic; he was choking to death.

I ran to my car and, as I did so, came face to face with a woman who was studying to be a chiropractor. I pushed her into the car and we headed up the road to the Indian lady's cottage, not very far away.

Arriving, we took in the situation quickly. The large dog was choking, but not fatally so. Soon we won his confidence enough for us to try to help him. The future chiropractor was able to slip her hand between his teeth — which took courage! — and discovered a small bone lodged in his throat, close enough to his mouth so she could reach it. In a minute she had dislodged it, and he coughed it out — then ran to his bowl to continue eating! The Indian lady had been too upset to take the action herself. Now, overcome with relief, she kissed the lady doctor and threw her arms impulsively around me. Her enmity was forgotten! In tears she explained how upset she had been over what was happening to her Bengali people in Bangladesh and how this had made her cranky and unreasonable. Arms around each other, we walked to the car. A full moon shone down on us, and thousands of stars hung in the immensity of the sky. Inwardly I marveled, offering my thanks profusely to Holy Mother for answering, so quickly, my hesitant prayer. What ingenuity, I thought! A solution of such complexity brought about so rapidly! There was a warmth in my heart and a gratitude I can still feel today.

Of course, the ugly word "coincidence" may now raise its head, and for those who must believe that way, I am perfectly willing to allow it. Only let me tell you of the second incident and an even more incomprehensible "coincidence."

As the summer drew to an end, and the coolness of September arrived, I began to think about leaving the Ashram. I was scheduled for one more talk on Sunday, September 29th and determined I would leave the following day. Shortly thereafter, I received a letter from San Francisco, inviting me to come for the annual ceremony at the local branch of a Japanese Church. I had stayed at the Home Church many times in Kyoto, Japan and felt very close to these people. Consequently, I wanted to go to San Francisco on September 28th, stay overnight at the Church, and be present for the ceremony on September 29th. But how could I do it? I had promised I would give my talk at the Ashram on the same day!

When I sat down to breakfast the following morning, after again reading my letter from San Francisco, I made some inquiries. I learned that a young scientist, who did not live at the Ashram, was scheduled to give a talk on September 22nd, so there did not seem to be any way I could change my engagement. Across from me sat a nun whose radiant face belied her seventy-odd years. I determined to explain the situation to her. "Sister—" I began, and then was interrupted by someone calling me to the phone. Mystified as to who would call me at the Ashram, I picked up the receiver and heard a voice I did not know, that of a young man. At first his name did not register. Then, surprised, I realized that it was the young scientist speaking on the other end.

"Mr. Stone," he said, "I know you are slated to speak at the Ashram on the 29th of this month, and I have promised to give my talk on the 22nd. However, I have a favor to ask. I have been invited to go on a backpacking trip down the Colorado River the weekend of the 22nd, and I would be very grateful to you if you would switch dates with me and give your talk on the 22nd instead of the 29th."

I was stunned. All I had said at breakfast was, "Sister" to my friend, the nun, and this unexpected event had swiftly followed. It meant I would be able to speak at the Ashram on the 22nd, drive to San Francisco, and be present for the Japanese Church Ceremony. How strange were the ways of the Mother with her children!

Coincidence? Two coincidences? It seemed to me I had become one of Mother's children in spite of myself, and that guidance has never left me since then.

How can we possibly make plans? How humble we are! We do nothing for ourselves, and yet everything happens! The momentum of the stay at the Ashram has taken me through several years now, bringing about all kinds of interesting teaching assignments involving two Universities and students from Japan, though I have no degrees. It is hard to see how we can refrain from gratitude, and is not gratitude a form of Devotion?

The Zen writer, Paul Reps, once confided in me that it was easy to be happy, that it actually took only fifteen seconds a day to insure happiness.

"What do you have to do, Paul?" I asked, somewhat skeptically.

"Every morning get up and say, three times: 'I am grateful, I give thanks!' " he replied.

I shook my head. "Too difficult, Paul," was my judgment. "You're asking too much — people won't do it. The maid didn't show up, it's income tax time, that fellow in the White House — there are any number of reasons every day for not doing it." He just smiled.

So Devotion cultures the Heart, and truthfully, nothing exists outside the heart. None of what happens is our own doing, and yet it is our own Karma that impels us. This is the great Mystery! How to reconcile the Divine Grace of Holy Mother with the cause-and-effect pattern we make for ourselves.

Since endless time men have been arguing over the Objects of their Faith. From this have come the Crusades, the Inquisition, all manner of Holy Wars, and bigotry of every sort. And yet the truth, from the Spiritual Point of View, is that the validity of the Object of Worship is not important. Where there is sincere, heartfelt belief, such devotion cultures the heart and completely changes the character of the believer. The Object of Worship becomes secondary to the Act of Worshipping.

In Indian history we have the famous Saint, Valmiki, who began as a highwayman and dacoit (outlaw). So sinful was he felt to be that his eventual Guru would not let him do Japa (repetition) of one of the names of the Lord, as was customary, but, instead, had him repeat the Holy Name of RAMA backwards, which came out as "MARA," name of the tempter corresponding to the Devil! And yet, by single-minded repetition of this dubious name, Valmiki reached one-pointedness of mind and Sainthood!

The Chinese and Japanese languages are wise in that they have two words, not one, for "heart." "Hsin" in Chinese and "Kokoro" in Japanese mean heart in the sense of Heart-Mind-Spirit, as opposed to the words describing the ordinary physical organ. We, too, speak of a "man with heart," and certainly mean something other than the man's central muscle pumping blood. It is in the sense of this heart-mind-spirit that we speak of the heart being cultured. Those who have meditated for a long time may very well have had experiences of "the cave of the heart" (the Upanishads speak of the Divine Person, the size of the thumb, in the cave of the heart), or even the realization that the throbbing, beating heart encompasses the Cosmos. At such a time, one wonders if there is anything outside the human heart, and that is a great awakening.

The aim of all true Spiritual Practice is One-Pointedness of Mind. Whether through Concentration and Meditative Disciplines, through single-minded devotion to a Spiritual Ideal, through control of breath and Prana (Vital Force), or through various physical practices such as Hatha Yoga, T'ai Chi Chih, and T'ai Chi Ch'uan, the ultimate goal is the completely focused mind not aware of a multiplicity of perceptions. The Japanese Buddhist chanting "Namu Myo Ho Ren Ge Kyo" or "Namu Amida Butsu," with nothing else in his heart, can reach this non-dual state of mind, as can the Sufi poet who sees only the Divine in all things and whose only perception is that of the Beloved. The philosopher and his speculations, the intellectual and his argument, and the worshipper of science who is besieged by the senses can never know the stillness of the one-pointed mind. It is not found in Variety, which the ordinary mind, so easily bored, constantly seeks. When we focus the rays of the sun through a magnifying glass, they can burn almost anything. Similarly, the completely focused mind, empty of all diversion, can accomplish almost anything. So whether we chant Mantras, pray to our version of the Deity, concentrate on a mindbreaking Koan, or endlessly make the single inquiry, "Who am I?", we are focusing the mind on just one thing. There is no turbulence, no competition going on.

"To a mind that is still the Universe surrenders!" says the poet. It is a state where there is just one active groove in the brain (vritti), and one-pointedness soon becomes no-pointedness, the Turiya or Fourth State of Consciousness spoken of by Indian Sages as the substratum of the other three. "Then the Spirit is an emptiness ready to receive all things," the poet continues.

But are we willing to pay the price to achieve such one-pointedness ("ekagra" in Sanskrit)? Do we have the necessary will for it? The habit energies of the mind (vashanas) cry out for amusement, and memories and daydreams rush in to distract the mind from its single poised status in the present. Very seldom do we live in the present; this is the difference between a Master, or Adept, and an ordinary man. Generally we are planning for the future or recreating the past. Placed here, we think about being there; doing this, we dream away our life. We constantly recreate exciting memories to let us know that we are alive. The photograph becomes more important than the original experience itself. So how can this unsteady mind be one-pointed and rest content in the present moment?

To play the piano well we must do finger exercises, practise reading music, learn to count and divide musical time correctly, and develop a concentration enabling us to express our inner resources in musical subtlety. On a sunny afternoon, how tempting it is to give up practising and go out to the fields to play! So easy to do! But to excel as a pianist, to eventually free ourselves from mere technique and achieve easily-coordinated spontaneity, we must overcome the urge to "cop out" and stay with the task at hand. A great musician is not one who is thinking of other things while he is playing! Those who have been fortunate enough to watch Toscanini conducting or Casals playing cello have had the feeling they were in church, so still and devout was the atmosphere. Music becomes religion, one-pointed religion, and we are deeply affected by it.

Young people frequently set out to do impossibly heroic tasks, then easily give them up because they can't be done. I remember one young man who was going to work all day at an Ashram, then cook most of the night at a pizza restaurant some distance away, and finally, get to a distant room to sleep by hitch-hiking through the streets in the early morning. He had no transportation. It was easy to see what would happen. In less than a week the whole routine broke down, and he spent some days in just catching up on his rest. This is not admirable but destructive. It is a pattern he will repeat and repeat. From a spiritual standpoint, we must set plausible goals and then follow them unwaveringly, not impossible objectives we can never fulfill.

I always tell T'ai Chi Ch'uan or Meditation students that I am not impressed by initial enthusiasm. The one who says, "How wonderful it is!" on the fifth day may have disappeared by the tenth day. It is steadfastness that impresses me, the one who sits meditation on his good days *and* on his bad days, or the one who practises T'ai Chi *every* morning, sleepy or not — these are the ones who achieve. And perseverance makes it that much easier as time elapses. Our practice becomes an important part of living and we prize it. "Practice and Enlightenment are one," says the Soto Zen Buddhist. Our practice becomes its own reward.

I have admired some who had great difficulty, originally, in sitting Zazen (cross-legged Zen meditation). It can be painful, and the pain makes the normally flighty mind even more jumpy — it becomes almost impossible to sit still for even two minutes, so how can the mind go to work to focus itself? But these people come back again and again, and gradually the difficulty works itself out. Having started from a difficult beginning, there is, naturally, a series of unconscious rewards waiting for them as they persevere. The Way to Reality is a lonely road, and we must travel it by ourselves. The passage down this road consists of putting one foot in front of the other. The longest journey begins with a single step!

CHAPTER 8

Serene face of old Japanese farm woman

A Spiritual Reminiscence

RAINY AFTERNOON
IN KYOTO

I t was a rainy day in Kyoto, with the mist hanging low over the Eastern mountain, much like a Hiroshige woodblock print. In my small, two-and-a-half-mat room in the Zen Temple, my meditation was often interrupted by the soft sound of the rain on the eaves of the Temple roof — a most reflective sound that, try as one might, often caused the mind to wander off in memory or dream.

By late afternoon, the haze had begun to lift from the mountain so that it was possible to see the green of the trees in the lower foothills. As I paused for a cup of green tea, sitting quietly in front of the hanging scroll that had just a circle on it, I could catch glimpses of Mount Hiei, to the east, through an opening in the screens that led to the temple garden. Whenever I saw Hiei-zan, I pictured it in flames, for in the sixteenth century, the great conqueror, Nobunaga, took an army up the steep slopes to the community of 20,000 people living in the Temple on the top and burned all the buildings to the ground, killing many thousands of Buddhists at the same time. He had warned the Temple authorities to stay out of politics — it is said they even had their own standing army! — and when his warning was ignored, he took the drastic step that ended the political influence of Buddhism in the old capital of Kyoto forever. So I always saw the mountaintop in flames in my mind's eye.

The rain had slowed to a drizzle and seemed about to clear entirely, so I walked out the Temple gate to stroll around in the clean, fresh smell of springtime. How greedily the earth drank the moisture! Everywhere the moss was soft underfoot.

I passed a small pond in which some boys, miraculously, had caught some tiny fish. I was surprised anything could live in the stagnant water. Now the fish, still breathing, were placed in plastic bags half-filled with water, and the boys ran off to

some other game, the bags swinging wildly as they ran. I idly wondered whether fish get seasick.

Passing a three-story pagoda, I noticed the Monk on top beginning to swing the huge bell, while chanting a Buddhist Sutra. "Kan Ji Zai Bo Sa Gyo Jin — " he began, fiercely intent on what he was doing. Down below, a boy and girl, wet from the rain, held hands, oblivious of a group of four students, wearing their school uniform tops, who were practising some four-part harmony under the shelter of the pagoda's overhang. And what were they singing, an old Japanese folksong? I could plainly hear "When the Saints go Marching In," sounding strange and foreign because they were mouthing unfamiliar sounds — they did not speak English.

On the main path, bicycles whizzed by with one child, sometimes two children, perched on the handlebars as fathers rode home from work to the evening meal. And though this was a Buddhist Temple, two old women were making offerings at a large Shinto shrine on the Temple grounds. Each person was, marvelously, only aware of his own activity, and there was a rare harmony to the overall picture.

Reaching the main street, Kurasama Doori, I was once again stimulated by the busy scene, so characteristic of an Oriental town. In the arcades, on the shopping malls, and in the open markets, wives were making last-minute purchases for that evening's dinner. Grandmas carried babies on their backs, and older children laughed and shouted, carrying schoolbooks under their arms. The younger ones wore yellow caps and had tiny packs on their backs. A Karate class, barefoot and clad in white, went swinging by, chanting as they ran. Small children played with tiny boats in the gutter where the water was high, oblivious of the speeding taxis. One man was stringing lights to an overhead wire, for that night there would be a local Street Fair, to which children would come in their bright kimonos, eating cotton candy, buying goldfish, leafing through magazines, and playing games of one sort or another. The surge of vitality was immense, and as always, fascinating.

Turning off the main street, I walked toward the riverbank. Here young men were playing baseball, couples were walking quietly, and a man stood on the bank relieving himself in the river, not far from a public restroom. Overhead the clouds turned lavender, a color I have seen in no other place, and there was just the trace of a distant muted sunset.

77

As I began to cross the narrow bridge — whose stones were old when the stones of Florence were being carved — I was delighted to meet my good friend, the University professor. Returning home from school, he had changed from western clothes to formal kimono and was now on his way to a nearby Shrine to pay respects to his Ancestors. I fell into step beside him, and we crossed the bridge together. A man was practising Kendo swordsmanship on the other side, making great guttural cries. He did not notice us as we walked by.

Soon we reached the gates of the Shrine, and, together, we paused to look at the multi-colored sky, not gaudy, not grotesque, but understated like a Japanese sumi painting.

"Kirei, desu ne!" murmured my friend, and I nodded — it was beautiful. There was no need for any answer. At that moment there was an irresistible rhythm to life, a renewing in the spring rain, that was beyond words; a feeling such as we often had after sitting hours of Zazen (Zen meditation) together in the Main Temple on special Buddhist days. And I remembered what one poet had said when he tried to describe the geese flying overhead at sunset — "I get lost in no-words."

CHAPTER 9

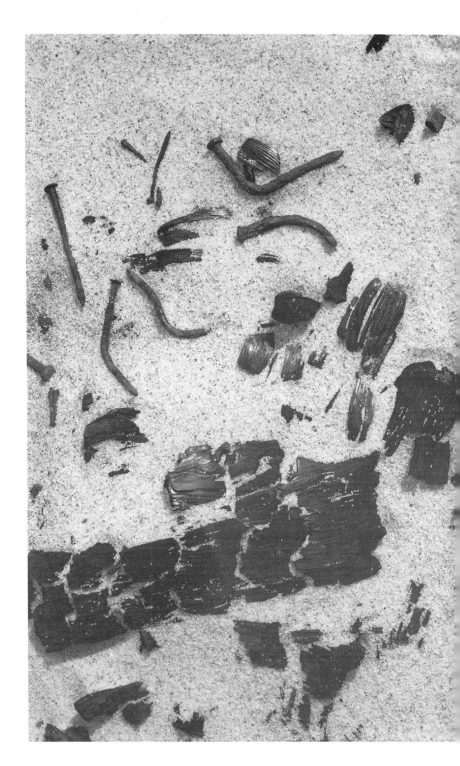

Rates of Transformation

THE GREAT SECRET —

Chi! Your Heritage

T he Indian people speak of Shakti, Kundalini, and Prana. Japanese call it "Ki" as in Aikido. And the Chinese speak of "Chi," the Vital Force, or Intrinsic Energy, that makes us one with the Universe. We are born with the "Chi" energy — indeed, we are the product of "Chi." And through our breath and Magnetism we accumulate Chi. T'ai Chi Ch'uan teachers say we store it in the bones and direct it from the Tan T'ien, two inches below the navel. The Zennists speak of "Your face before you were born." When we function spontaneously — what else can this be but the chi? Those who practise the Yogic Pranayama are dealing with the breath, but real Pranayama practice concerns the "Chi" (or Prana) associated with the breath. The Indian Sage has said that this Force — all the energy in the Cosmos — is the Reality. Our ephemeral selves come and go, are born and die — but was there ever a beginning to the Vital Flow? One of the New Religions in Japan worships electricity. This is not as foolish as it seems; is not electricity a Universal Manifestation of this Chi?

A T'ai Chi Ch'uan or T'ai Chi Chih adept, who has practised for many years so that the force has accumulated, trembles in his fingers when he performs. He is not nervous; the flow of Vital Energy pours through him, like a faucet turned on. One of my Chinese Master's most advanced students, himself a well-known teacher, gave a demonstration of T'ai Chi Ch'uan in Taiwan, and while he was doing so, high-speed color photographs were taken. When the pictures were developed, there was great surprise to see a curving bluish light coming from just below the navel. This parallels the evidence I once saw in a series of twenty photographs taken automatically over a period of hours while a Tibetan Yogi went into deepest meditation, Samadhi. By the tenth photograph, light had begun to appear from below the Yogi's navel, and by the eighteenth, nineteenth, and twentieth pictures, there was nothing but light perceptible. There seems to be no way these automatically-taken time exposures could have been faked.

One time when the author was performing T'ai Chi Ch'uan and T'ai Chi Chih in a fenced yard behind his house near the ocean, an unexpected visitor entered and cried out in astonishment.

"What's the matter?" I asked, alarmed.

"I see a lavender light all around you, like a mist!" the visitor, a man in his sixties, exclaimed.

Mystics, and all who meditate a great deal, are usually familiar with the amorphous lavender-blue that shimmers before their eyes after, or sometimes during, meditation. I have seen it form a Mandala, going in and out of focus like a picture projected on a screen. This is a manifestation of the Chi energy, and it is possible that the seeming blue of the sky is due to this energy. Those who practise various Chi Kung exercises — T'ai Chi Ch'uan, T'ai Chi Chih, Nei Kung — come to realize that what appears to be space is a vast continuum of energy. And the secret of activating it, one of the great secrets of life, has to do with CIRCULARITY.

When we hear of healing by laying-on-of-hands, or by some similar method (such as the very effective focusing of this force in the Johrei practice of the Church of World Messianity, called Sekai Ku Sei Kyo in Japan), we know it is a use of this great Chi Energy.

It has often been reported that Mahatma Gandhi, as he grew older, slept with young women — not with sexual motives in mind, for he insisted on strict Brahmacharya (continence) from all his followers — but in order to use an ancient Tantric method of renewing vitality. (I know of no way to actually authenticate this story about Gandhi.) The Church of World Messianity has used it to facilitate the growth of fruits and vegetables in its model farm near San Diego. I have eaten them and can attest to the success of the method, where no fertilizers or insecticides were used.

This development of the Intrinsic Energy is one of the greatest secrets of Life, used by Chinese Taoists (who balanced the Yang and the Yin, the substantial and insubstantial divisions of this Force) in order to achieve great longevity. The true Alchemy was spiritual and had to do with developing immortality by these methods, but was misunderstood to mean

82

the creation of gold from base metals because of the symbols the Taoists used. Those who are puzzled by such treatises as *The Secret of the Golden Flower* would do well to keep such meaning in mind when reading this and other esoteric works.

In Tibet and Northern India when a village has been frequently attacked by dacoits, the inhabitants go in search of a Holy Man of the highest calibre. It is felt that, if he will, he can draw a psychic circle around the village, into which those with evil intent cannot venture. This, of course, is the Chi Force used constructively by a Master. We must remember that, for every Master, there are a hundred charlatans. Paul Reps once wrote me that "India is full of Saints and Aints." The Aints, of course, far outnumber the Saints.

It is felt that the healings by Jesus, reported in the New Testament, were examples of a Master's use of this Vital Energy. It must be remembered that, in Indian Philosophy, there are basically only two essentials — Akasha (space) and prana or Chi (all force or energy). Before the modern scientific era this would not have been believed; people would have pointed to "inert matter." But since Einstein, we know there is no inert substance, and that what seems to be mass is really energy (the basis of the Atom Bomb). Twenty-five hundred years ago Buddhism proclaimed this, and went even further. If what was declared is true, one day this energy will be found to be Thought.

Eastern adepts, particularly in China, take the Chi Energy on a mentally-guided tour through the eight meridian channels of the body, freeing blockage, toning circulation, and greatly energizing the metabolism. This is in complete accord with acupuncture, which works through the major and minor channels (meridians) of the body in a way not yet known to Western medicine, but which is now proving out in experiments. After all, Chinese medicine is much, much older than the symptomatic medicine of the west. Acupuncture reaches the inner organs through outer terminal endings, sometimes using needles and sometimes deep heat (moxibustion) to correct the Yin-Yang imbalance and bring relief to the patient.

Those who have practised the T'ai Chi disciplines, or Chi Kung, know that the flow is started by thought, followed by the Chi (very often causing a trembling of the hands), and

finally, culminates with the blood. This is one basis of self-healing. When there is an ache in the body, the adept will place his thought (consciousness) right in the center of the pain rather than trying to avoid it. This will tend to bring the Prana (Chi) to that spot, as the flow of Chi follows the concentration. Then the blood will flow to the same place. In a few minutes it may be difficult to find the pain.

T'ai Chi Ch'uan practicers usually keep their concentration two inches below the navel, or if this is too difficult, in the soles of the feet (called the Bubbling Spring by the Chinese). After a period of practice — and performers tend to gain energy as they progress, rather than tiring — an internal heat develops, and the practicer begins to feel warm, without perspiration. Knowing this will happen, on cold nights when there is snow or ice outside, I have usually cautioned pupils not to go out in their shirtsleeves; the night had not turned warmer, but their metabolism had changed.

T'ai Chi students, as well as Zen meditators, are usually very thirsty after practice. The flow of Chi has dried up most of the internal aqueous excess (the cause of much overweight and illness, according to the Chinese), and the thirst is natural. The students must be careful not to drink anything cold, as this would be a shock to the inner organs, and hot tea, which is also used in Zen to fight drowsiness, is the most effective drink. Many people have seen demonstrations by Karate or Aikido experts, in which a rather puny older man will break a log or a concrete block with his bare fist; this is a well-known phenomenon. (Indeed, in Japan, a group of Adepts gathered together to quickly demolish a whole building in this manner.) Onlookers are puzzled as to how a tiny man, of no great muscular development, can perform such a feat. It is to be noted that, as he draws himself up, the performer gives a sudden cry, which activates the Chi stored in the bones and Tan T'ien, and then does the astounding cutting operation with his hand. It has nothing to do with muscular power; it is a functioning of the Chi energy.

There is a well-known story about a Chinese Judo expert, weighing around 200 pounds, who went with a bigger friend, also an Adept, to visit a tiny Aikido Master in his seventies.

"All my life I have been hearing about the power of the Chi," began the Chinese, meanwhile noting the fragile appearance of the old man. "Would it be asking too much for you to give a practical demonstration of it?"

The little man thought for a moment. "I'll tell you what," he answered. "You and your friend attack me from opposite sides of the room and throw me down. And do me the honor of not taking it easy with me!"

The two big men looked at each other. "We'll kill the little fellow!" was what they undoubtedly thought. Hastily they conferred, whispering together.

"You flip the little man and I'll catch him before he hits the mat — we don't want to hurt him!" suggested the Chinese man, and the other readily agreed.

The two big men, both Adepts, separated and slowly came at the tiny Master. There were many spectators, and they held their breaths, hoping the little man would not be injured.

Suddenly the two big men burst into action from opposite directions, both lunging at the little fellow. The next thing apparent to the watching spectators was incredible — the Chinese man was lying on the floor ten feet away, dazed, his glasses off, looking, as he put it, for the freight train that had hit him. His friend had been slammed against the wall — hard — and a speck of blood appeared on his nostrils. What is most remarkable is that nobody had seen the Master move!

The above is a spectacular demonstration of mastery of the Chi, and many, many similar stories have been told in the Orient. When one begins to practise the Chi Kung disciplines, he feels a thrust of force through himself, and after a while, it begins to resemble an internal bath, as though one has turned a faucet and caused the flow. The effects on Health and Longevity are dynamic.

To those who have been in Northern India — or Tibet and Nepal — the sight of Sadhus (Holy Men) wandering in the coldest weather, wearing nothing but a loincloth, is a common one. A freezing traveler will wonder how they can maintain body heat. At 4:00 a.m. they may bathe in the upper portions of the Ganges, and the mountain reaches of that great river are cold at such an hour! These Adepts, of course, have developed the Inner Heat and know how to circulate it. Japanese monks have performed the same feat under waterfalls in coldest weather, chipping away the ice. I know of one case where the monk had not developed the ability, however. After only a minute in the water, he withdrew, screaming. Later the same evening he developed a high fever and eventually had to be sent home from the monastery.

This ability to generate the Inner Heat is one of the prime practices of Tibetan Tantric Buddhism — and also of the White and Black Magicians in that unusual country. It has been said that this Dumo Heat (Dumo is the Central Channel, called Tummo in China) is "the essence of magic play." Long and rigorous training is necessary to pass this barrier and develop the desired inner flow. Finding that many western doctors had doubts of the ability of the body to change itself in this manner, the author determined to personally test the authenticity of the training. Without a teacher to help, he spent one year on the practice and finally had the amazing experience with a flow that lasted at least twelve hours, through the night, and made sleep impossible, so intense was the heat and the manifestation of energy. Thinking he would be tired, with no sleep, the author arose the next day to a feeling of extraordinary vigor and well-being. It was a unique experience, but there were various unpleasant internal effects during the year, and I would not advise it for most people.

Hatha Yoga, Pranayama, T'ai Chi Ch'uan, T'ai Chi Chih, the secret Nei Kung and other Chi Kung exercises, Kundalini Yoga, and various other disciplines are ways to arouse and circulate this Vital Force, the Intrinsic Energy. "To unite the Chi in me with the Cosmic Chi" is the way one scholar defined the goal of the disciplines dealing with this Force. So one surmounts his individuality and reunites with the Great Force of the Universe.

Hakuin Zenji, one of the two greatest Zen Masters in Japanese history, tells of his trip to the mountains, when he was young, to find a great Sage (Sennin) there. We must remember that the Japanese, and particularly Zennists, are noted for understatement. In Hakuin's case, also, we are dealing with one of the greatest Religious teachers the Orient has known. Was he apt to be a liar or an exaggerator? Yet he wrote that, when he found the great Mountain Sage in his cave, during the coldest part of the winter, the Sage was wearing little clothing and had been without food for a month or two! The unbearable chill of those mountains had turned the vest-like covering completely stiff, yet the Sennin felt no cold and knew no hunger! There were many stories about his age, which was estimated to be amazingly advanced, yet when he walked down the mountain to guide Hakuin to a nearby stream so Hakuin would not get lost, there was no hesitation in the older man's step (he wore clogs) and no weariness in his demeanor. Hakuin referred to him as "The Perfect Man, like the heroes of old." The Sennin explained all this by, "What is it but the power of the Chi Energy?"

It would be well if the West becomes more than dimly aware of this Vital Force (how to stimulate and use it) and its part in building Health, Joy, and Longevity. I know of no greater, more important Secret.

It would seem fitting to close this chapter on the Great Secret by quoting the Chinese Scholar — T'ai Chi Master, Professor Huang Wen-Shan. He says:

"...we seem to realize that, in the Universe, there is an ever-active, ever-creative Life, and an inexhaustible source of Energy-Life and Energy which are made available to Mankind when a fitting stage of development is achieved. *It is particularly significant that it has a great Reverence for Life.*"

In referring to the practices by which one masters this Force, Professor Huang continues: "It must be pointed out that this particular exercise, with its emphasis on spiritual value...,is not to be compared with those systems emphasizing only the training of sinews and muscles. Exercise, in all its branches, can bring the greatest benefit to Mankind only if man recognizes a unifying principle for its creative ingenuity. Indeed, the highest dimension of human exercise concerns itself with the world view and moral spiritual purposes of life."

So we find that the Science of the Chi, the well-kept great Secret of Sages, is essentially spiritual in nature as, indeed, is all Life. Probably there will be scoffers, though none can deny the Vital Force of Life. But those who have learned — and practised — the disciplines know there is something great and incomprehensible, and its flow brings a Joy to their lives.

CHAPTER 10

To the U.S.A.

TWO MISSIONARY CHURCHES

We seldom think of missionaries coming *to* the United States. Yet, just as India is sending Gurus to America, other countries, such as Japan, are exporting churches. Whereas the Gurus come on their own, with some backing or by representing a group of followers and teaching a particular spiritual discipline, the churches tend to be very tightly organized, and their incursion into this country has usually been the result of much planning. Invariably, they are solid financially (unlike some of the Gurus) and soon develop Boards of Directors, legal corps, and other characteristics of what is often aptly called "Churchianity."

Two of the Japanese Church groups with which I have been intimately acquainted are Sekai Kyusei Kyo (called "Church of World Messianity" in the United States) and Tenrikyo, particularly the large Kotoku sect within the latter.

Since the death of its Founder, the Sekai Kyusei Kyo has been slowly fading away in Japan, but it has been prospering in the United States. Most people here think of it as the "Healing Church," and, as the Church of World Messianity, it has been sending missionaries out from the Los Angeles headquarters to spread the word of the Johrei Practice and its healing properties. The missionary ministers to the United States have worked hard to master English conversation, and as a result, the rapidly-growing membership of the Church is about evenly divided between Oriental and Caucasian. This is highly unusual and speaks well for the planning and adaptation abilities of the Church authorities. Most Japanese imports, such as Jodo Shinshu and Tenrikyo, make their appeal to second and third generation Japanese-Americans, and the Churches and Church ceremonies remain highly Japanese in character. Zen Buddhism, which is not a Church, is an exception, the heavy meditation practice and lack of worship appealing much more to Westerners, particularly intellectuals, than to those of Japanese descent.

Although the Church of World Messianity has fostered a worthwhile blending of two cultures, the leadership remains strongly in Japanese hands and is guided from the Home Church headquarters in Atami, Japan. For example: the really excellent translations of the Founder's words by the original American head, Reverend Higuchi, go through an unusually complicated formula to make sure they agree with the viewpoint at the Home Office in Japan. After being laboriously translated into good English, they must then be changed back into Japanese so that the officials in Atami can check that nothing has been added and the Party Line has been rigidly followed. After approval, these words are again translated into English, not an easy task because the colorful Founder, Okada Mokichi (known as "Meishu-Sama"), wrote most of his work in poetic form. This has been admirably maintained in the transfer to English, and the poetic words of the Founder are quite impressive, even in the new Language.

This two-way path, the growth in the West and gradual expiration in Japan, will probably create problems in the future. Though most present-day Japanese, judging by my own experience, have not heard of Sekai Kyusei Kyo, the Japanese organization is enormously rich and has really impressive properties in Atami and near Hakone. In fact, these properties, including classic gardens and an extensive museum, are the prototype for the coming "Paradise on Earth." However, as the American membership grows, there may soon be some restiveness on the part of Caucasian members, who may want to govern their own Church and break away from some Oriental customs, such as praying to Shinto gods (in the adopted "Amatsu Norito" prayer) and offering food to the dead. There may even come a time when the Western Church wishes to splinter off from the tight Japanese rule, though at present, a very firm grip is held by the Home Church.

The History and Development of this Church, which has had many names since the Founder seceded from the Omotokyo religion and founded his own Church, is fascinating but not as important as the really different practice of Johrei, which

92

young Americans are beginning to practise and enjoy. Meishu-Sama, the Founder, discarded healing by use of a wooden spoon (as taught by Omotokyo) and began to use the hands as healing channels. This actually is a use of the Pranic force, but highly unusual as there is no contact between the Channel and the one receiving Johrei. The Founder had a revelation in which his writing of the Chinese character for "Light" (HIKARI in Japanese), worn around the neck of the Channel as a talisman, would afford great power to raise spiritual vibration and, at the same time, heal physical disease. It was revealed that there is a Spiritual World, in which all events take place before they are consummated in this physical sphere (almost Platonic in concept). The raising of the spiritual vibration dissolves clouds in the Spiritual Realm, with their accompanying accumulation of toxins in the physical body, and the greater purity leads to rapid healings here on earth. During his lifetime, O Hikarisama ("Mr. Light," as the Founder, Meishu-Sama, was known), was paid enormous sums of money to perform his "healings," and this was the basis of the beautiful facilities, Japanese gardens, and Art treasures in Atami. The Founder felt that Beauty is a way to Spirituality, and the ready accessibility of the uniquely Japanese Art treasures was much appreciated by the people of Japan after the War.

When the Founder became seriously ill and, refusing to see a doctor, failed in his efforts to heal himself, the Church was dealt a serious blow of credibility, and the gradual decline in Japan probably dates from the time of Meishu-Sama's death.

What appeals to many young Westerners is the fact that there really is no need for Doctrine and dogma in this Church. Johrei is received — and given — in silence. It is joyous, and no words are needed. If you ask the average person to sit quietly on a backless stool for thirty minutes, you will find it an impossibility; five minutes will be too much, and he will become restless. Yet, when people come under the "light of Johrei" for the first time, they not only sit quietly for a comparatively long period (perhaps ten or twelve minutes facing the Channel and ten or twelve minutes with the back turned), but seem genuinely regretful when the time is up. Some even sneak back for a second Johrei!

Aside from a definite feeling of well-being, the only thing felt is a sensation of heat in the spot on which the Channel is focusing, and not all people feel this. Some psychics have claimed to see light coming from the outspread palm of the one giving the Johrei. The author, on receiving Johrei (he also gave it for some years), usually goes into a state much like that of deep meditation without any effort, and there is a definitely pleasant feeling, as though worries have evaporated.

The late Reverend Freeman used to go to Mental Institutions to channel Johrei to the patients, and he told me that the most disturbed and violent ones instantly became quiet when he raised his hand to them.

One woman Channel was extremely psychic, and she had the unfortunate property of picking up the recipient's symptoms as soon as the latter sat across from her. One time a visitor sat down in front of her to receive Johrei for the first time, and this psychic Channel immediately screamed with pain! She had no way of knowing it, but the newcomer was suffering from kidney stones, and she at once picked up the painful symptoms. After that, the Church cut down on the length of time she was allowed to channel, as it seemed injurious to her health.

There are some who say the presence of the talisman worn around the neck is more for protection against picking up the Karmic symptoms of the other than for help in stimulating the healing power of the "Light." Those who give Johrei often feel the heat in the palm of the channeling hand, just as the sitter feels it in his body.

It is partly because of the Karmic consequences that the author stopped giving Johrei, though whenever he is in Los Angeles, he likes to visit the Church, say "hello" to friends, and receive Johrei from a Channel. (There is, of course, no charge for this, but a small donation may be made on the Altar.) Some strange and interesting experiences have taken place there. It seems that the strength of Johrei varies widely, depending on who is giving it, though this is not a part of the teachings, and when one is a Channel, he might possibly induce very unusual experiences in others, sometimes seemingly beyond time and space.

It is the teaching of the Church that a giant cataclysm — Armageddon — is building up, not hard to believe in this world today. As the "Light gets stronger," evil and violence will be forced to the surface. Those who have "raised their spiritual vibration" will have nothing to fear, but others will suffer greatly. The aftermath of the eventual holocaust, when much of Mankind will disappear, will be "Paradise" or Heaven on Earth. (This is not, of course, a new teaching, and it directly conflicts with the idea that the Kingdom of Heaven is within.)

Because the practice of Johrei depends on feeling and not on words (we already have too many of those!), it has great appeal. If the Church will minimize Christian and Shinto prayers and the seemingly irresistible lure of "Churchianity," it should have solid growth in the West, even while fading in materialistic Japan. The hymn singing and stereotyped sermons will place this Church in the same category with every other church, and the competition is enormous. On the other hand, Johrei stands alone and is the real strength of World Messianity, providing it is not made into some sort of magic play. The idea of "raising spiritual vibration" is a laudable one, and Johrei seems well-suited to accomplishing this aim. Moreover, the fact that one is giving and one receiving, in Johrei practice, is unique, and supposedly, the one giving receives benefit just as does the one receiving. I have seen many impressive demonstrations of the power of Johrei! Indeed, it would be nice if we had "Johrei Stations" in all cities, quite apart from church dogma, where weary workers and other disillusioned people could stop during the day for twenty or thirty minutes to receive the revitalizing benefits of Johrei.

The following are a few quotes from the writings of the Founder of Sekai Kyusei Kyo, Okada Mokichi (Meishu-Sama):

Unification

The Old Age of Darkness was an age of counter-clockwise vibration which caused centrifugal movement.

Because of this vibration, disintegration occurred to some degree in practically every field of the old civilization — scientific, religions, etc. — and all became divided into smaller and ever-smaller segments.

The New Age of Light has a completely opposite, clockwise vibration, which causes centripetal action. This vibration brings about unity and clarity, so all things become welded into one harmonious body, with all segments focused on the center. This is the true state of the great, worldwide changeover, which has become clear in its actions to everybody who looks for signs of the New Age.

God's Plan

Since the beginning
Of His Creation, the great
God of Light has had
His Plan for establishing
Paradise on earth for man.

Johrei

Purifying earth
Of its clouded condition
Can best be achieved
Through channeling
God's great Light,
Lifeline of True salvation.

The story of Tenrikyo is almost diametrically opposed to that of Sekai Kyusei Kyo. A huge power in Japan, claiming five million adherents in the world, Tenri has a vast and well-organized missionary department and has missionary churches as far away as the African Congo! Tenri City, which houses Tenrikyo's headquarters, is located in Nara, has its own railroad station, and is much larger than Vatican City. It boasts one of the great anthropological museums of the East, a near million-volume library with many rare items, and its own University, well-known for its athletic teams. The shops, theatres, city hall, and market places make this a busy metropolis, and it could be called the "Mecca" for all Tenrikyo members throughout the world.

Tenrikyo, which means "Heavenly Wisdom," has as its nerve center a large compound within Tenri City. I have been there on special days when 300,000 pilgrims, carrying their own food (except for hot tea), have come to this compound, and I have heard the old-fashioned court music played outside by 2,000 musicians — absolutely overpowering. Tenri, which is 125 years old, was founded by a woman, MIKI, after a Divine revelation, which caused her to give away all her possessions, reducing her and her family to abject poverty. She suffered incredible hardships during her lifetime and was jailed many times before religious persecution in Japan became a thing of the past.

96

The main compound takes up more than one square kilometer in Tenri City, and it contains JIBA, the spot where the world was supposedly created. In the center of JIBA is the KANRODAI. According to the teaching, one day the "Sweet Dew" (KANRO) will pour down from Heaven (the KANRODAI is roofless) and all Mankind will turn to Jiba as its home. MIKI had taught that the true life expectancy of man is 115 years, and after the Sweet Dew has fallen, all people will become members of Tenrikyo and live to that ripe age. (MIKI herself, the Foundress, died at the age of ninety.)

There are two enormous Chinese-style buildings connected by meticulously dusted hallways seemingly the length of football fields. These are the center of religious ceremonies, which begin each day (as at all Tenrikyo churches) at sunrise and are repeated at approximately sunset.

Behind these large buildings are the huge dormitories where Westerners and black Africans are sometimes seen. Every new member of Tenrikyo (including children or grandchildren of member families) must come to this place to hear the Doctrine of Tenrikyo nine times. (Pregnancy takes nine months, and it is felt that hearing the doctrine nine times will cause it to come alive, like a baby, in the minds of the listeners — it is interesting that "nine" is the positive number in Chinese teaching.) Here the fascinating dance, chanting, and hand movements (O Tsutome, symbolizing sweeping away of the "Dust") are learned by the newcomers. Having lived for long periods of time in a Church Center where these movements, the singing, the offering of food to the dead, and other rituals take place, the author can attest to the power of the services. Tenrikyo believes in YOKIGURASHI — Joyous Life — and it is easy to see the joy and devotion in the faces of the believers who regularly perform these rites. If only scoffers had the same reward!

Though they do not speak English,the fine people at my "home" base shout "Joyous Life!" at the end of each service. They do not mean one should try for a joyous existence; they mean it is the *duty* of each one to live joyously, that one has no right to spread gloom and negativism.

The concept of "Dust," which is not exactly Sin, is an important one in Tenrikyo, as it is in many Japanese religions, and reminds us of the famous Zen poem about keeping the bright Mirror free of dust. This HOKORI, the Dust, is of eight

The author with Church dignitaries in front of the beautiful Tenrikyo Kotoku Tea House.

The author teaching a class at Tenrikyo Kotoku Church. The head of 220 branches of the Church, Mr. Hayashi, at far end.

kinds: Greed, Stinginess, Partiality, Hatred, Animosity, Anger, Covetousness, and Arrogance. One of the ways to wipe out these stains is to offer HINOSHIKAN (voluntary free labor), and countless man-hours of such voluntary work are responsible for a good deal of the enormous construction in the Tenri City compound.

From the time the newcomer finishes his training at the Tenri headquarters and returns to his home, his connection with the Church life is more intimate than what we know in the West. His social life will be built around his home Church, and he will enjoy being there, with occasional pilgrimages to Tenri City itself. His children will go to the home Church to practise Flower Arrangement (KEBANA), Tea Ceremony (CHA-NO-YU), Classic Dancing (ODORI), and other Japanese Cultural Arts. Youthful musicians, often beginners, will practise with the Youth Band, which will lead the procession of this Church's followers as they parade through the streets of Tenri City on special festival days — often playing the U.S. Marine Marching Song! These children will occasionally bring their equivalent of sleeping bags to the Church so they can spend the night together in the Main Sanctuary, bathing and eating together in a festive atmosphere for two days. It all makes for a strong feeling of joy and solidarity in the Church atmosphere. This is heightened by the willingness of the ministers to discuss any problems of everyday life with the laity, offering sympathetic ears to troubled members.

Tenri teaches that the body is merely borrowed from God the Parent, and that the mind should be kept as innocent as that of a three-year-old child. Although the body must be returned, there is free will and each is given the right to develop his own mental attitudes. Accumulation of the Dusts mentioned previously means suffering. But to true believers, Painless Childbirth is promised. (Many Tenri mothers have solemnly testified to me that this is true, and I have seen expectant mothers working on their hands and knees up to the very time of birth without being in any way attended by a doctor.) Many faith healings are reported, as in all religions. The author has frequently witnessed these benefits, and, sleeping upstairs near the Ancestor Room, I have heard ceremonies almost like exorcism rites during the night when an old man was sick.

Originally, God the Parent was called TSUKI-HI (Tsuki equals Moon and Hi means Sun), and a frequent pictorial representation is that of the MOON-SUN God shining on endless muddy waters before the first men (who were only three inches tall) were created. There is much that is reminiscent of Shinto in the Creation myths and doctrinal teachings of Tenri, with Shinto gods actively referred to. In addition, some accretions from Buddhism and Christianity are readily apparent. For instance, though native Japanese religions spend little time discussing afterdeath states, there is a reference to the fact that, when one dies (gives back the borrowed body), he will immediately be reborn in another body. This conflicts with the traditional Japanese view that, when one dies, he becomes a KAMI (minor god or spirit) who hangs around the house of his descendants, protecting the UJI GAMI (Clan) from which he came. Further, in some of the Shinto-like ceremonies of Tenrikyo, food is offered to the ancestors (prostrations are made in three directions to KAMI SAMA, the Supreme God; to the Foundress, MIKI; and to the Ancestors), which presupposes that they are still around as spirits and have not taken new bodies. This rather fuzzy version of reincarnation, as well as the doctrine of INNEN (Karma), shows a definite Buddhist influence somewhat foreign to the tenets of Tenri itself.

While my experience with the other Church, Sekai Kyusei Kyo, has been principally in the West, my most vivid memories of Tenrikyo are those of the exceedingly happy times I have spent at the Kotoku Branch Main Church in Kyoto, near Doshisha University.

The Head of this Division, comprising about 220 branches, is Reverend Jutaro Hayashi who has wisely kept his people living the old-fashioned way. This is a definte source of strength. One steps backward in time when he goes from ultra-modern Tokyo to the Church community of Reverend Hayashi. The bath is heated by a fire, patiently tended outside (sometimes in the snow) for hours, as there is no running hot water for the thirty or forty people (men, women, and children) making up the permanent population of the Church. Laundry is processed by hand over rocks outside in a small "interior" garden. The cooking is on old-fashioned brick; everybody sleeps on comfortable FUTONS on the tatami matted floor; five-thirty a.m. is Reveille time seven days a week; and all toilets, with one recent exception, are flush to the floor in Japanese style. Perhaps a word about the OFURO (Japanese bath, which is such an important ritual in the old-style life), the laundry women, and my experience with the advent of modern toiletry at the Church would be interesting.

Being a guest, it was my privilege (or, unfortunately, duty) to enter one of the two baths first, along with high officials of the Church. This meant it would be scalding hot, and since the same bathwater would be used by all inhabitants of the little community, one did not wish to dilute it with cold water at 5:30 p.m. when it would still be in active use till at least 11:00 p.m.

Japanese bathrooms are ingenious, the floors being concave and slanting to a drain in the center. Thus one bathes outside the tiled tub (big enough for two or three people) before stepping into the steaming water, which has been heated by fire, with wooden planks fitted over the tub to hold the heat in. After disrobing in the anteroom, one enters the bathroom carrying a three-inch-high stool and shivering mightily. (After all, the window in the bathroom has been left open so the fire tender outside can reach in frequently to test the temperature of the water under the wooden covers!) A bucket is used to scoop water out of the tub, and this is poured over one's naked self (the chill in the body leaves very quickly under the scalding water!), after which one squats on the stool and soaps himself into a great lather. (If one is also going to shave, he does it squatting and uses a small mirror a few feet off the floor.) Then, another dousing with water from the bucket and one is clean enough to step into the tub. (No one would think of fouling the water, so it will still be clean after six hours when the old women are using it.)

Paul Reps taught me to step into the tub quickly and stand absolutely still — otherwise the steaming water will really hurt. After a minute or two of getting used to the heat, one gets up enough nerve to lie down in the tub. There is the initial shock, and then — bliss! The relaxation is unutterable and one will not be cold again for at least three or four hours. Naturally, the temptation is to luxuriate as long as possible in the tub, being careful not to fall getting out, as the heat makes one giddy. For some of the hard-working people, this is the only time of relaxation during the day, and the desire is to prolong it, though one knows others are waiting to have their bath. The "Ofuro" bath is a ritual in Japan, and inexpensive public baths are scattered throughout streets of the cities so that no one goes dirty. This is a custom we might give some thought to.

One time, as my stay was coming to an end at the Tenrikyo Kotoku Church headquarters in Kyoto, I determined to give a useful gift to the hard-working women who washed the community's clothes, and everything else, by hand on the rocks in the tiny interior garden. I suggested to the wise Head of the Church that I would like to buy an electric washing machine for the women, expecting that he would be pleased at the propsect of acquiring such a time-saving device.

He frowned. "Then what will the women do?" he asked, to my surprise. Nevertheless, he consented to my inquiring of the women if they would like such a gift. They unanimously voted against it! They enjoyed their work, the occasional cup of tea, the camaraderie, conversation with the others, and also the sense of being useful.

I have often admired the Japanese characteristic of enjoying work, and nowhere is it more in evidence than at the Church. When I would go with my good friend, Reverend Takahashi, to his family's ultra-modern barber shop, I would be aware that everyone worked from 7:30 a.m. to 7:30 p.m. — yet, when the shop had closed for the night, the barbers, assistants, and masseuses often sat around drinking tea and chatting, obviously in no hurry to leave. (After having a shampoo, a massage, and a special razor cut by the talented head barber, I would be served coffee, tea, cakes, and ice cream in an anteroom. When I tried to pay for the extraordinary services, everybody would look pained and turn away. Finally, as I left, they would all walk out into the street with me, bowing and saying "sayonara," and asking my pardon for the poor service!)

It had not been easy for the Western visitor to get used to the Japanese toilet, and this must have been noticed by the sensitive and considerate people. At any rate, after lunch one day (eating sitting on the floor mats in the kitchen), I was asked to step into a small inner room. Much to my surprise, there was a toilet bowl with seat standing in the center of the room, not connected to anything. "What in the world — ?" I wondered, but soon found out.

All the inhabitants gathered at the doors, beaming my way. Obviously something was expected of me. "Aren't you going to try it?" someone asked. I was shocked. "Sit down, see if it's big enough," urged one minister.

I wondered if I was supposed to lower my trousers. It was an embarrassing moment, but there was no help for it. I did as requested — it was a trifle small.

Everybody cheered. I waved my hands in triumph. Later that day an older man, who was a master carpenter, began to install the apparatus in a small closet-like chamber, with beautiful tilework around the base of the stool, but making no allowance at all for any flushing mechanism. When he was finished, he had just raised the hole in the floor to a higher, more comfortable level (which was very welcome).

Of course, having lived there among these people, it is easy to remember many, many such incidents. Returning home about midnight, from an evening spent working with scholars, I would stand in the intermittent rain while waiting for someone to answer my ring at the main gate. Three women — who had undoubtedly been sleeping — would appear quickly, one carrying an umbrella to hold over my head, one a pot of tea and a few crackers, and the third holding a lantern so I would not bump my head on the very low ceilings. And after accompanying me to my room, they would sit and chat about my evening while I had the tea and cookies. The next morning when I asked them whether they weren't sleepy, they would smile and nod agreeably — of course they were sleepy! Big joke.

So, how can I express my gratitude for the joy I have found in the simple, natural life there? I really love these people.

As missionary churches, the strengths of these two may be reversed. Because Tenrikyo's Shinto-like doctrine and well-developed dogma are aimed primarily at the Japanese temperament, the missionary branches in the western part of America (Los Angeles, San Francisco, Vancouver, and other localities) have, as members, mostly those of Japanese descent. Unless the authorities come to better understand the Western way of thinking, this will tend to limit the growth of the Church here, as there aren't that many Japanese-Americans. On the other hand, Sekai Kyusei Kyo (the Church of World Messianity), while very small in Japan compared to

Tenrikyo, has prepared its missionary ministers well; they speak good conversational English and somewhat understand the Caucasian outlook. Too, JOHREI supplants the need for a complex doctrine and easily appeals to the feelings. Consequently, more Westerners than second or third generation Japanese are joining the Church of World Messianity, and missionaries are spreading the practice of JOHREI up and down the Pacific Coast and as far east as Colorado. There is a good prospect of continued growth by this Church in America, no matter what happens to the Home Church in Japan.

Because the leaders of the Kotoku branch of Tenrikyo are dynamic and persuasive, this branch may be able to break away from the purely Japanese atmosphere now prevalent and, as younger members of the leading family learn English, may bring the Church outlook to a more Universal point of view. It is hard to see how the good will and joyous behavior of the people can be transplanted here, however; ours is a different way of life. The Church will have to change dramatically to succeed with Caucasians in America.

It will be interesting to look back ten years from now to see what inroads the two missionary churches have made. Japanese products are now a way of life in this country. Will the two churches be as successful as SONY and TOYOTA?

The Altar in Tenrikyo Main Sanctuary

CHAPTER 11

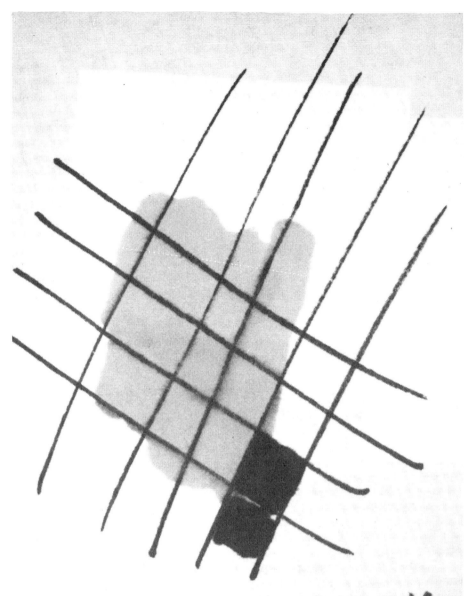

POEMS OF
INNER MEANING

I MUST REMEMBER TO FORGET.

ONLY THE HUMAN HEART HEARS THE FALLING SNOW.

107

UNDER TENDER SNOW, EARTH LIES DEEP IN MEDITATION.

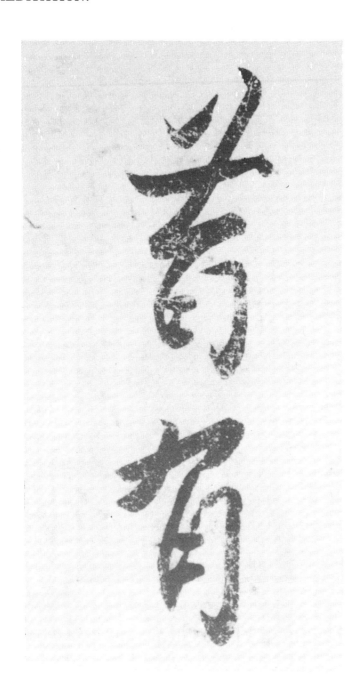

SUFFER THE LEAVES TO FALL (IN AUTUMN).

FIRST FROST, PUMPKIN-STILLNESS.

EACH ACCORDING TO HIS NEED.

NURTURE THE NOWNESS!

WAITING, WE DO NOT WAIT ALONE.
BETTER TO BE WITHOUT HOPE.
THAT WHICH IS WITHOUT ASPECT
  HAS NO BECOMING.

MEDITATION: NON-SITTING (NO ONE HOME).

GOING, WE RETURN.
  WE MEET OURSELVES COMING BACK!

WE LIVE! WE DIE!
TO FIND REAL MEANING EVERY MOMENT,
      WE LAUGH! WE CRY!

NO NEED TO PLANT.   WHAT IS IS IN ABUNDANCE.
WHAT IS NOT, SHALL NEVER BE.
NO NEED TO SUFFER!
WHAT IS OURS
        CANNOT BE TAKEN AWAY.

Along the Ganges in Benares, the Holy City

CRYING OUT —
        THE SOUND OF GROWING, SPLASH OF SUNSHINE,
            DEEP SONG OF DEW AND GRASS.

WISE MEN ARE ONLY WISE WHEN THERE ARE FOOLS.

AFTER PASSION
    SHYLY COMES
        COMPASSION!

A DEAD BRANCH, A WITHERED LEAF
SUDDEN RECOLLECTION!

DO NOT WORSHIP NATURE:
NATURE IS A CLOAK.
DO NOT "SEARCH FOR GOD."
GOD CANNOT BE "FOUND."
THE EYE DOES NOT SEE THE EYE,
THE TONGUE CANNOT TASTE THE TONGUE;
THE POOR MAN CANNOT "BECOME POOR."
BLESSED BE THOSE WHO KNOW
ALL ARE SINGING THE GLORY OF CREATION!

113

NO ONE KNOWS MY TRUE NAME.   MY TRUE NAME IS ____.

NEVER WANDERING FAR FROM OURSELVES.

FROM THE SOUND OF TIRES ON THE PAVEMENT,
WE RECONSTRUCT THE PASSING CAR.

ILLUSION OF PAIN,
    THE PAIN OF ILLUSION.

WHO CALLS?   WHO ANSWERS?

RIVER OF JOY,
    SILENTLY OVERFLOWING.

UN-FRAGMENTED.

115

DO NOT PUSH.
IT WILL COME OF ITS OWN ACCORD
IF IT IS MEANT TO COME AT ALL.
HOW WE STRUGGLE TO MANIPULATE
THAT WHICH CANNOT BE MANIPULATED!

ONLY ONE WHO LIVES LIKE ME
CAN UNDERSTAND MY LIFE.

SUFFERING, SPLITTING, CRYING OUT IN PAIN —
HOW JOYOUS ALL WE CHILDREN ARE!

SOMEWHERE —
    IN THE MIDDLE OF
        NOWHERE.

WHEN WE ARE STILL,
    WE HEAR THE WORLDS TURNING DEEP INSIDE,
    VIBRATING IN SOUNDLESS SOUND.

SELLING THE MOUNTAIN FOR A DOLLAR,
BUYING THE PRAIRIE FOR A DIME —
CUTTING THE LONG-LIVED FOREST,
WE DIE A LITTLE!

THE MIST HAS SETTLED, AND WE HAVE LOST THE ROAD.
PAI!

PLANTING IN THE SPRINGTIME, WE HARVEST IN THE
FALL.

SPREAD ROUND, THE HARVEST OF THE SUMMER NOON.
TO BE IS TO RECEIVE; TO KNOW IS TO REJOICE!

PLEASURE IS REACTION; JOY IS WITHOUT CAUSE.

THE MELTING APRIL SNOW STILL CLINGS TO LIFE!

GLOSSARY

ASANA — Means "Posture," not only Yogic Postures, but any position one takes. For instance, the way we sit in Meditation is an "ASANA."

ASHRAM (or ASHRAMA) — Originally a forest retreat where one lived simply under the tutelage of a great Teacher. It has come to mean a Commune of sorts, with Spiritual leanings, and many are springing up in the West.

BODHISATTVA — In Mahayana (one of the two divisions of Buddhism), the ideal is the man who takes a vow to save all others (all sentient beings) before saving himself. This lofty saviour is called Bodhisattva. (Bodhi means Enlightenment, Sat means Being, and the Tva indicates "essence of." He is the Essence of Enlightened Being.) A Bodhisattva is just one step short of being a BUDDHA.

BUDDHISM — The Religion or series of Religions derived from the teachings of the Buddha, the Perfected One. Lord Buddha lived in Northeast India 2500 years ago, was born a prince, and left the Royal Life to become a renunciate. His eventual Complete Enlightenment resulted in his teaching of the principles of Anicca (Impermanence), Dukkha (Suffering of all beings), and An-Atman (no ego-entity, no individual self or soul). The various schools that developed from his initial teaching, which was designed to enable followers to reach "Nirvana" (literally, extinction, the merging of the seeming-individual into the Universal) are all parts of Buddhism, a Religion that has many divisions and many sects. Buddhism is known as an "Atheistic Religion" as it does not posit a Creator-God.

DHYANA-SAMADHI — DHYANA means Deep Meditation, in which the Mind has merged with its object, bringing about One-Pointedness of Mind (ekagra). Continued practice of Dhyana (Meditation) eventually can result in SAMADHI, the Superconscious State.

HATHA YOGA — One of the eight steps in the great Raja Yoga chain that leads to full Enlightenment. By itself, HATHA (meaning SUN-MOON) YOGA is often called the "Yoga of

Physical Perfection." It mainly consists of the practice of ASANAS (Yogic postures) and should not be thought of as "exercise."

HINOKISHIN — Free labor offered by Tenrikyo followers to their Church, resulting in much merit. Tremendous building jobs have been accomplished with this free labor, and when there is no task to be done, visitors to the Tenri City headquarters often do symbolic carrying of dirt as a substitute. It is a familiar sight in Tenri City.

HOKORI — The "dust" that has been piled on the soul through incorrect conduct and thought. This concept of "dust" obscuring the essential purity of the self is a familiar one in both Chinese and Japanese Religion.

INDIAN BHAKTI — BHAKTI means Devotion. One who worships God or a Guru (personal teacher) is performing BHAKTI. It is the Way of Devotion as opposed to Physical Yoga, Yoga of Good Deeds, etc.

INNEN — This Japanese word roughly means "Karma," the doctrine of Cause and Effect (so noticeable in Buddhism and Indian Religions). It means we harvest the rewards, good or bad, for our deeds and thoughts ("As ye sow, so shall ye reap"), and attitudes play an important part in the development of our "Innen."

JEN — Often translated as "Human-Heartedness," a keystone of the teachings of the Sage, Confucius.

JIBA — There is a place within Tenri City, the Tenrikyo headquarters in the city of Nara, that is called JIBA and is said, by Tenrikyo teachers, to be the place where the first men were created. They predict it will one day be the Spiritual Home for all mankind.

JOHREI — A Practice of the Japanese Sekai Kyusei Kyo Religion. It consists of focusing the open palm of the hand, without touching, on an area of the body of the one sitting for Johrei. Generally considered as a Healing Technique, the Founder of Sekai Kyusei Kyo said it was a way to "raise spiritual vibration." While giving Johrei, the one doing so always wears around his neck a "Focal Point," a talisman with the Chinese character for "Light" written on it. He usually wears the talisman at other times as well.

KANRODAI — Also known as the "Sweet Dew Stand," this is a spot in the Main Sanctuary of the Tenrikyo headquarters where the "Sweet Dew" (almost "manna") will pour down from Heaven one day. When this KANRO, or "Sweet Dew" pours down into a wooden vessel on top of the KANRODAI (which is a wooden column), all mankind will become one under the Tenrikyo banner, it is said.

KOAN — This comes from the Chinese words "KUNG AN." Without going into the semantic derivation (about "case"), it is used today to describe the problem given to Rinzai Zen students to concentrate on. This problem is usually taken from a famous encounter or dialogue, such as the one where a Monk asked the Master Joshu if a dog has Buddha-Nature. Joshu answered "MU," a Chinese word with many meanings (usually "Negation"). This "MU" has become a Koan on which many generations of Zen aspirants have pondered. In "Sanzen," private meeting with the Master, they try to express their understanding of the Koan, really to "manifest the answer." Such answer must be approved by the Master before they go on to another Koan, and this sometimes takes years to accomplish.

MAHARISHI MAHESH YOGI — A disciple of the Shankaracharya of Northern India, he went out on his own after the death of his Master, came to the West, and began to teach what he called "Transcendental Meditation" (essentially Indian Manasika Japa). Now he has several organizations in the West and a few thousand pupils who serve as initiators. Maharishi received great publicity during the period he was teaching the Beatles, and some of this has backfired. However, his organizations have made inroads in the Universities of the U.S. and, in general, have found representation in many countries of the world. Maharishi himself is a sweet man who feels he has a mission to perform.

MANTRA — A Mantra is a Name of God or a syllable that has great power ("Chaitanya" in Sanskrit). Supposedly a great RISHI (Sage) discovered the Mantra after years of austerity and gave it to the world. Usually an aspirant receives "his" Mantra from his teacher and uses it for Meditation and for endless Repetition (JAPA). In India it is said that Repetition of the Lord's Name or Names is the one way to God Realization in this decadent period (Kali Yuga). It is not true that a Mantra is a "magic" sound, but the constant repetition of the Lord's name is sweet to the mind and gradually makes grooves in the brain until the Mind becomes one-pointed in this lofty sound.

MIKI — Born in 1798, Nakayama Miki became the Foundress of Tenrikyo after first being a devout member of the Pure Land Sect (Jodo Shinshu) of Japanese Buddhism. She later deliberately impoverished herself and her family on a "direct order from God" and suffered much persecution during her lifetime, including being jailed. There is a special shrine to her in the main buildings of the Tenrikyo headquarters in Tenri City.

NIYAMA — This might be referred to as "Attitudes." NIYAMA means to observe five things: Physical and Mental Purity, the Practice of being content with one's lot, Austerity in living circumstances, Surrender to the Object of Meditation, and Study of Scriptures and Yogic writings of Self-Knowledge.

PATANJALI — Often called the "Father of Yoga," the great Patanjali is the one who codified the Science into the eight steps of Raja Yoga.

PAUL REPS — Reps is a unique man who became known for his collection called *Zen Flesh, Zen Bones* (written with the monk, Senzaki), and other books, such as the picture-poem book called *Zen Telegrams*. He lived in Japan for a number of years and has long been a world traveler.

PRAJNA — Means "Wisdom," pointing at the innate Wisdom that is within each of us and does not have to be acquired. It does not refer to acquisition of book knowledge. Modern

Zen, since Hui Neng's time, has stressed spontaneous manifestation of this Innate Wisdom.

PRANAYAMA — One of the "outer" steps in Raja Yoga. This is really the Science of the Vital Force (PRANA), rather than practice of Breath Control, as many believe. It is roughly equivalent to the Science of Chi Kung in China. Since Indian Philosophy believes the Universe is composed of only two things — Energy (Prana, Shakti, or Kundalini) and Space (Akasha), the importance of the control of the flow of Intrinsic Energy can well be realized.

PRATYAHARA — Another of the "outer" steps in Raja Yoga, it means withdrawal of the senses from their field of objects so that the attention is turned within, resulting in Meditation and Samadhi. It is by this practice — through such disciplines as "Yoganidra" — that the Yogi is able to make himself immune to pain and even to control the heartbeat.

RAJA YOGA — Patanjali codified all Yogas into eight steps, five "outer" and three "inner." This is called Raja Yoga or the Kingly Yoga. The ultimate aim of Raja Yoga is to attain SAMADHI, the superconscious state. Patanjali said that the purpose of Yoga is to "Inhibit or Suppress Mental Modifications."

SAMADHI — The so-called "Superconscious State," resulting from deepest Meditation, and the last step in Raja Yoga. Here there is no world, no sense stimuli, no sense of "I-ness." Great Yogis say there are two kinds of Samadhi, SAVIKALPAKA (the lesser of the two, in which the Mind still retains Impressions), and the Ultimate, NIRVIKALPAKA (where all distinctions have faded and only Consciousness itself is "perceived" or realized).

SATORI — A Japanese term deriving from the verb "Satoru," meaning "to Realize." This experience ("WU" in Chinese) is the sudden, overpowering Realization of Truth, often accompanied by a breaking out of perspiration and other physical manifestations. It is said to be the greatest Joy. It is not true that one Satori is final, however. Hakuin Zenji and other Masters speak of Major and Minor Satori experiences. These eventually result in Kensho, the state of complete Enlightenment. Some Zen Masters speak of two kinds of Satori, DAIGO (the state of Oneness, of complete merging and non-differentiation) and SHOGO (coming back to the everyday world and observing one's own Satori so one can become a social human being again).

SILA — One of the three "Baskets" of Buddhism, the first observance, stressing correct conduct.

SRIMATA GAYATRI DEVI — This is the name of the Head of the Ananda Ashrams in America. She is a direct Spiritual descendant of the great Ramakrishna. Gayatri refers to the Divinity in the Sun and Devi means Goddess. Srimata is an honorific.

T'AI CHI CHIH — Little known in the East (please see the author's book called *T'ai Chi Chih, Joy Thru Movement*), this is a series of easily-learned movements that help the CHI (Intrinsic Energy) to flow, circulate, and be balanced. Has the same benefits as T'ai Chi Ch'uan but is much easier to learn.

T'AI CHI CH'UAN — A Chinese Yoga, often called a Moving Meditation with 108 movements. Balancing the Yin and Yang (Negative and Positive forces), this form is said to bring health, serenity, and longevity. Many people in China practise this "Cosmic Dance," and it is becoming very popular in the West. Many of the so-called Martial Arts derive from it.

TAOISM — Chinese Philosophy, usually traced to the great Sage, Lao Tzu, which advised a "natural" Way of flowing with Reality, the TAO (or Supreme Ultimate). Later it became a Religion and changed considerably, but it may be seen in its purity in the writings of the philosopher, Chuang Tzu and in the *Tao Te Ching* of Lao Tzu. Taoism was not interested in future states of existence but believed the real meaning can be found here and now in the sweat and tears of this world. It was decidedly not a pessimistic philosophy.

TEH — Perhaps "Power of Inner Sincerity" might fit this difficult word. Mencius, the great Confucian of China, said, "What is whispered in the ear is heard 1000 miles away," and so saying, he was pointing at this power. Confucius felt the Superior Man must have both Human-Heartedness and the Power of Inner Sincerity.

TENRIKYO — A major Japanese Religion about 100 years old. While it seems somewhat Shinto in character, Tenrikyo is considered completely independent from other religions.

VEDANTA — One of the six schools of Philosophy in India (called Darshanas), Vedanta today is probably the reigning Philosophic thought in that religious country. True Vedanta, as described by the great Shankara, would be a teaching of Non-Duality, but these days, many different schools of thought in India call themselves "Vedanta," including those that advocate a Way of Devotion (necessarily dualistic). Vedanta, which comes from the Vedas (most sacred scriptures of India), has also been defined as "Direct knowledge of Supreme Consciousness," which must be realized through practise.

YAMA — One of the two preliminary steps of Raja Yoga. YAMA consists of five observances or vows: Non-injury, Non-stealing, Non-covetousness, Thinking and Speaking only Truth, and Brahmacharya (continence or sexual abstinence).

ZAZEN — This is the Zen practice of "Sitting," in Zen Meditation posture. However, Zen teachers say brushing the teeth and eating rice can also be part of Zazen, so anything done with mind concentrated in the Buddhist manner is ZAZEN.

ZEN — The CH'AN School of Buddhism in China derived from the teaching of Dhyana (Meditation) in India, supposedly coming to China in the person of Bodhidharma, the First Chinese Patriarch. (Actually, he was Indian.) The word ZEN is simply the Japanese reading of the Chinese character for CH'AN. So Zen is a sect of Buddhism, usually thought of as the "Meditation Sect" or the "Mind Sect," and it feels it is perpetuating the true Buddhism, without regard for Scriptures and other written word, through "Transmission of Mind."

ZEN MASTER DOGEN — Dogen Zenji was the founder of Soto Zen in Japan, a sect that now has about 15,000 temples. Born in 1200, Dogen made the dangerous trip to China to imbibe the true Buddhist Transmission, feeling that Buddhism in Japan lacked much. He returned to the Japanese Islands in 1227 and brought back some of the teachings of the Ts'ao Tung sect, later founding the great Eihei-ji, the temple that became the center of Soto teaching in Japan. Dogen was one of Japan's greatest philosophers, as well as a true Zen Master.